Name _____ Date _____

# Place Value Through Hundred Thousands

---

**You can write numbers in different ways.**
**312,501 can be written in:**

**Standard Form**     Use digits—**312,501**

**Word Form**     Use words—**three hundred twelve thousand, five hundred one**

**Short Word Form**     Use digits and words—**312 thousand, 501**

**Expanded Form**     Use digits to show the value of each place
**300,000 + 10,000 + 2,000 + 500 + 1 = (3 × 100,000) + (1 × 10,000) +**
**(2 × 1,000) + (5 × 100) + (1 × 1)**

---

**Write each number in standard form.**

1. 415 thousand, 25

2. 800,000 + 4,000 + 60 + 2

3. 100,000 + 900 + 20 + 3

_____      _____      _____

4. three hundred forty-seven thousand, one hundred five _____

**Write the value of the underlined digit in short word form.**

5. 1<u>3</u>7,294

6. <u>5</u>63,089

7. 426,<u>7</u>18

_____      _____      _____

**Write the number in word form, short word form, and in expanded form.**

8. 702,946 _____

---

**Problem Solving**

**Show Your Work**

9. At times, the earth is two hundred thirty-eight thousand, eight hundred fifty-seven miles from the moon. Write this number in standard form.

_____

1

**Use with text pages 4–5.**

# Place Value and Exponents

---

**You can use exponents to write numbers.**

$10^4 = 10 \times 10 \times 10 \times 10 = 10,000$

**You can use exponents to write numbers in expanded form.**

$(8 \times 10^5) + (7 \times 10^4) + (2 \times 10^3) + (5 \times 10^2) + (9 \times 10^1) + (6 \times 10^0) = 872,596$

---

**Use exponents to write each number in expanded form.**

**1.** 19,742 _____

**2.** 617,945 _____

**3.** 56,067 _____

**Write each number in standard form.**

**4.** $(4 \times 10^5) + (9 \times 10^4) + (5 \times 10^3) + (7 \times 10^2) + (6 \times 10^1) + (3 \times 10^0)$ _____

**5.** $(2 \times 10^4) + (1 \times 10^3) + (8 \times 10^2) + (5 \times 10^1) + (1 \times 10^0)$ _____

**What is the value of *n* in each equation?**

**6.** $60,000 = 6 \times 10^n$ _____     **7.** $5^2 \times 3 = n$ _____

## Problem Solving

**Show Your Work**

**8.** Are $10^0$ and $2^0$ equal? Why or why not?

_____

Use with text pages 6–7.

# Place Value Through Hundred Billions

---

**Different Ways to Write Numbers.**

| | |
|---|---|
| **Standard Form** | 20,650,389,260 |
| **Word Form** | twenty billion, six hundred fifty million, three hundred eighty-nine thousand, two hundred sixty |
| **Short Word Form** | 20 billion, 650 million, 389 thousand, 260 |
| **Expanded Form** | $(2 \times 10,000,000,000) + (6 \times 100,000,000) + (5 \times 10,000,000) +$ $(3 \times 100,000) + (8 \times 10,000) + (9 \times 1,000) + (2 \times 100) + (6 \times 10)$ |
| **Expanded Form with Exponents** | $(2 \times 10^{10}) + (6 \times 10^8) + (5 \times 10^7) + (3 \times 10^5) +$ $(8 \times 10^4) + (9 \times 10^3) + (2 \times 10^2) + (6 \times 10^1)$ |

---

**Write each number in standard form.**

1. 42 billion, 126 million, 3 thousand, 13 __42,126,003,013__

2. seven hundred fifteen billion, two hundred four million, one hundred two _____

3. $(6 \times 10^9) + (3 \times 10^7) + (1 \times 10^6) + (7 \times 10^4) + (2 \times 10^3) + (9 \times 10^1)$ __6,031,072,090__

**Write the value of the underlined digit in short word form.**

4. 813,709,426 _____

5. 68,091,352,426 __50 thousand__

**Use exponents to write the number in expanded form.**

6. 91,726,482 _____

**Find the value of n.**

7. $n - 1 = 999,999,999$ __1,000,000,000__

8. $n + 2 = 10,000,000$ _____

---

## Problem Solving

**Show Your Work**

9. The population of China in the year 2000 was estimated at 1,261,832,000. The population of the U.S. in 2000 was estimated at 275,563,000. How much greater was the population of China than that of the U.S.?

__986,269,000__

**Use with text pages 8–9.**

# Compare, Order, and Round Whole Numbers

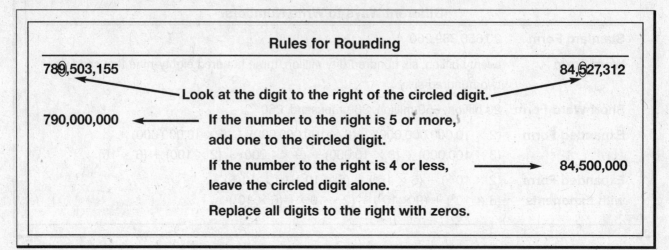

**Compare. Write >, <, or = for each ◯.**

1. 24,981 ◯> 24,810

2. 734,556 ◯ 734,655

3. 45,813,540 ◯< 48,513,450

4. 2,198,070 ◯ 2,189,007

**Order each set of numbers from greatest to least.**

5. 9,254; 9,542; 9,515

   9,542; 9515; 9,254

6. 18,229; 18,209; 18,299

   _____

**Round to the place indicated by the underlined digit.**

7. 22,0<u>1</u>5,899  22,020,000

8. 9<u>9</u>6,842,176 _____

**Write a number for the missing digit that will make the inequality true.**

9. 8_3,174 < 893,173

   Any digit less than 9

10. 265,_13 > 265,631

**Equations. Find the correct value of n.**

11. n + 900 = 10,000   9,100

12. 10,000 − n = 9,990

## Problem Solving

**Show Your Work**

13. A toy company had a profit of $259,304 this year and $254,509 last year. Which profit was greater? Explain.

    This year's profit is greater because
    259,000 > 254,000

**Use with text pages 10–13.**

# Place Value Through Thousandths

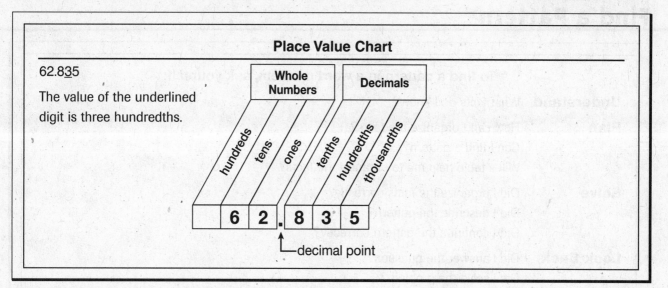

**Place Value Chart**

62.835

The value of the underlined digit is three hundredths.

|  | Whole Numbers |  |  |  | Decimals |  |
|---|---|---|---|---|---|---|
|  | hundreds | tens | ones | tenths | hundredths | thousandths |
|  | 6 | 2 | . 8 | 3 | 5 |  |

↑ decimal point

**Write each in standard form.**

1. twelve and fifty-four hundredths  12.54

2. six and sixteen thousandths  6.006

3. one hundred sixty-two thousandths  ~~0.62~~
0.162

4. twenty and five hundredths  20.05

**Write each decimal in words.**

5. 23.6  twenty-three and six tenths

6. 8.002  eight and two thousandths

7. 10.01  ten and one hundredth

8. 2.112  two and one hundred twelve thousandths

**Write the value of the underlined digit in words.**

9. 8.147  seven thousandths

10. 515.42  4 hundredths

## Problem Solving

11. A laser measured Karen's height as forty-nine and seventeen thousandths inches. Write this height as a decimal.

**Show Your Work**

49.017 inches

**Use with text pages 14–15.**

# Problem-Solving Strategy: Find a Pattern

| | **To find a pattern in a word problem, ask yourself:** |
|---|---|
| **Understand** | What facts do I know? |
| **Plan** | How can I organize the facts? |
| | Can I find a pattern? |
| | Will a table help me to organize the facts? |
| **Solve** | Did I organize the facts correctly? |
| | Did I describe the pattern? |
| | Did I continue the pattern correctly? |
| **Look Back** | Did I answer the question? |
| | Did I solve the problem? |

**Find a pattern to solve each problem.**

**Show Your Work**

1. Mr. Santos is driving from Atlanta, Georgia to Phoenix, Arizona. On the first day, he drove 183 miles. He drove 213 miles on the second day, and 243 miles on the third day. If this pattern continues, how far will Mr. Santos drive on the fifth day?

   Explain your thinking. _____

   _____

   _____

2. Oakdale School is sponsoring a canned food drive. In the first week of the drive, the students collected 638 cans. They collected 698 cans in the second week and 758 cans in the third week. If the students continue to collect cans at this rate, in which week will they collect more than 1,000 cans?

   Explain your thinking. _____

   _____

   _____

**Use with text pages 16–19.**

# Compare, Order, and Round Decimals

---

### Compare Decimals

To compare 0.56 and 0.6:

- Align the decimal points    0.56

                          0.6

                         ↑

- Compare the digits until they are different.

   $0.56 < 0.6$

---

**Compare. Write >, <, or = for each ◯.**

**1.** $7.23 \bigcirc 7.2$        **2.** $0.145 \bigcirc 0.45$        **3.** $0.081 \bigcirc 0.81$

**4.** $0.9 \bigcirc 0.900$        **5.** $6.22 \bigcirc 0.62$        **6.** $5.073 \bigcirc 5.307$

**Order the numbers from greatest to least.**

**7.** 6.2; 6.02; 6 _____      **8.** 5.32; 0.325; 2.53 _____

**9.** 1.09; 11.9. 19.1 _____      **10.** 3.18; 0.83; 3.8 _____

**Round to the place of the underlined digit.**

**11.** 7.1<u>5</u>6 _____      **12.** 34.<u>2</u>77 _____      **13.** 0.<u>9</u>81 _____

**Compare. Write >, <, or = for each ◯, given $a = 0.465$, $b = 0.8$, $c = 0.06$, and $d = 1$.**

**14.** $a \bigcirc c$        **15.** $d \bigcirc b$        **16.** $a \bigcirc b$

## Problem Solving

**Show Your Work**

**17.** Precious jewels are measured in carats. A jeweler has a ruby weighing 0.627 carats, a diamond weighing 0.82 carats, and a pearl weighing 0.092 carats. List the jewels in order from heaviest to lightest.

_____

**Use with text pages 20–23.**

Name _____ Date _____

# Algebra: Expressions and Addition Properties

| You can write an algebraic expression for a word phrase. |
|---|
| **Word Phrase**    a number decreased by 5 |
| ↓      ↓      ↓ |
| **Algebraic Expression**    $n$    $-$    5 |

**Write an algebraic expression for each word phrase.**

**1.** add 12 to a number

**2.** 3 less than a number

**3.** 14 plus a number

_____

_____

_____

**4.** 20 more than a number

**5.** take 16 from a number

**6.** a number reduced by 5

_____

_____

_____

**Translate each algebraic expression into words.**

**7.** $k + 9$

**8.** $25 - a$

**9.** $x - 7$

_____

_____

_____

**10.** $11 + b$

**11.** $h - 13$

**12.** $50 + c$

_____

_____

_____

**Evaluate each expression when $b = 18$. Then write $>$, $<$, or $=$ to compare the expressions.**

**13.** $b - 0 \bigcirc 36 - b$

**14.** $24 - b \bigcirc b - 8$

**15.** $7 + b \bigcirc b + 7$

**16.** $(b + 5) + 4 \bigcirc b + (5 + 4)$

## Problem Solving

**17.** In Mrs. Campbell's class, there are 17 boys and some girls. Write an algebraic expression that describes the number of students in the class.

_____

**Show Your Work**

8

**Use with text pages 28–31.**

# Estimate Sums and Differences

| Ways to Estimate a Sum or Difference | | |
|---|---|---|
| Round to the greatest place. | Round to a lesser place. | Use front-end estimation. |
| **3,278** rounds to  3,000 | 3,278 rounds to  3,300 | 3,278 rounds to  300 |
| **+1,634** rounds to  +2,000 | +1,634 rounds to  +1,600 | +1,634 rounds to  +600 |
| 5,000 | 4,900 | 4,000  +  900 = 4,900 |

**Estimate. Tell which method you used.**

1.  746
   +683

2.  957
   −512

3.  8,315
   +4,879

4.  6,114
   −2,352

5.  4,085
   +7,601

6.  7,020
   −1,986

7.  57,308 − 29,554

8.  $78.31 + $64.09

**Estimate. Decide whether the sum is closer to 50 or 100.**

9. 33 + 24

10. 54 + 46

11. 67 + 27

12. $41 + $13

_____  _____  _____  _____

## Problem Solving

**Show Your Work**

13. A drama club sold 768 tickets to Friday's
   show and 922 tickets to Saturday's
   show. About how many tickets did the
   club sell altogether?

_____

9

**Use with text pages 32–33.**

Name _____  Date _____

# Add and Subtract Whole Numbers

Regroup when adding or subtracting whole numbers.

$$
\begin{array}{r}
\overset{1\ 1\ 1}{5\,7,8\,4\,3} \\
+\,2\,4,1\,6\,5 \\
\hline
8\,2,0\,0\,8
\end{array}
\qquad
\begin{array}{r}
\overset{7\ 9\ 9\ 10}{1\,\cancel{8},\cancel{0}\,\cancel{0}\,\cancel{0}} \\
-\,1\,2,8\,4\,3 \\
\hline
5,1\,5\,7
\end{array}
$$

**Add or subtract. Check that your answer is reasonable.**

1.  5,087
    +4,395

2.  8,914
    +6,382

3.  41,948
    + 8,655

4.  57,209
    +25,863

5.  868
    −599

6.  4,000
    −2,731

7.  84,306
    −55,704

8.  10,000
    − 3,629

9. 58,745 + 19,622

_____

10. 30,134 − 24,868

_____

**Find each sum or difference when $n = 3,000,000$ and $s = 250$.**

11. $n + 7$

_____

12. $n + 7,000$

_____

13. $n + 7,000,000$

_____

14. $1,000 - s$

_____

15. $10,000 - s$

_____

## Problem Solving

**Show Your Work**

16. During the summer, the population of Spring Lake is 30,155. During the winter months, the population drops to 13,876. How many people spend only the summer months in Spring Lake?

_____

**Use with text pages 34–37.**

# Add and Subtract Greater Numbers

When adding or subtracting greater numbers, choose either mental math, paper and pencil, estimation, a calculator, or a computer to solve the problem.

---

**If you use paper and pencil, make sure to line up the ones digits.**

4,871,506 + 1,349,005

$$\begin{array}{r} {}^{1\ 1\ 1\ \ \ 1} \\ 4,871,506 \\ +\ 1,349,005 \\ \hline 6,220,511 \end{array}$$

200,000 − 65,815

$$\begin{array}{r} {}^{1\ 9\ 9\ 9\ 9\ 10} \\ \cancel{2}\cancel{0}\cancel{0},\cancel{0}\cancel{0}\cancel{0} \\ -\ \ \ \ 65,815 \\ \hline 134,185 \end{array}$$

---

**If you estimate, round to the greatest place.**

4,871,506 rounds to → 5,000,000
+1,349,005 rounds to → +1,000,000
Estimate 6,000,000

200,000 rounds to → 200,000
− 65,815 rounds to → − 70,000
Estimate 130,000

---

**Add or subtract. Tell which method you used.**

1. 708,214
   +290,528
   **998,742**

2. 516,000
   − 25,772

3. 346,572
   +628,719
   **975,291**

4. 6,050,100
   −1,342,800

5. 815,090
   +667,401
   **1,482,491**

6. 275,000
   −125,000

7. 4,553,409
   +3,177,200
   **7,730,609**

8. 6,927,000
   −2,000,000

9. 5,700,000 − 65,500
   **5,634,500**

10. 360,000 + 640,000
    _____

## Problem Solving

Use the table for Problem 11.

11. What is the estimated total population of the four towns listed to the right? Explain how you know.

    **220,000**

| Town | Population | |
|------|-----------|---|
| Oakdale | 87,430 | **90,000** |
| Pleasantville | 54,905 | **50,000** |
| Springfield | 42,887 | **40,000** |
| Valley View | 36,523 | **40,000** |

**Use with text pages 38–39.**

Name _____ Date _____

# Algebra: Mental Math: Addition and Subtraction Equations

---

**You can make a model to write and solve an equation.**

Today, Aki read 6 more pages of her book than she read yesterday.
Today she read 26 pages. How many pages did she read yesterday?

| Today 26 pages | |
|---|---|
| Yesterday: $n$ | Difference: 6 |

**Yesterday + difference = today**

$$n \ + \ 6 \ = \ 26$$
$$n \ = \ 20$$

Aki read 20 pages yesterday.

---

**Write the equation shown by the model. Use mental math to solve the equation.**

**1.**

| 28 children | |
|---|---|
| $b$ | 17 children |

_____

**2.**

| 54 | |
|---|---|
| 29 | $k$ |

_____

**Use mental math to solve the equation. Use models if necessary.**

**3.** $g + 7 = 32$

**4.** $84 - m = 52$

**5.** $21 + v = 41$

**6.** $r - 56 = 90$

_____  _____  _____  _____

**7.** $88 + j = 97$

**8.** $s - 47 = 83$

**9.** $\$2 + m = \$5$

**10.** $a - 100 = 0$

_____  _____  _____  _____

## Problem Solving

**Write an equation to solve the problem.**

**Show Your Work**

**11.** Shannon had a coupon for popcorn at the movies. The original price of the popcorn was $3.10. Shannon only had to pay $1.75. What was the value of the coupon?

_____

**Use with text pages 40–41.**

# Problem-Solving Decision:
# Relevant Information

Use with text page 42.

---

**Ask Yourself**

- What is the question?
- What do I need to know?
- Which is the important information in the problem?
- Do I have enough information?
- Is there information in the problem that I don't need?
- Did I answer the question?
- Did I solve the problem?

---

**Draw a model to solve. Show your work. If there is not enough information, tell what information is needed.**

**Show Your Work**

1. Mrs. Davis went to the show with $35. She bought a picture frame for $5 and a wreath for $12. She also bought lunch at the show. How much money did Mrs. Davis spend?

   _____

   _____

   _____

2. During the first two days of the show, 1,238 raffle tickets were sold. If 665 tickets were sold on the first day, how many tickets were sold on the second day?

   _____

   _____

   _____

Use with text page 42.

# Algebra: Expressions and Multiplication Properties

| Properties of Multiplication | | |
|---|---|---|
| Commutative Property | $a \times b = b \times a$ | $6 \times 7 = 7 \times 6$ |
| Associative Property | $a \times (b \times c) = (a \times b) \times c$ | $2 \times (3 \times 5) = (2 \times 3) \times 5$ |
| Identity Property | $a \times 1 = a$ | $8 \times 1 = 8$ |
| Zero Property | $a \times 0 = 0$ | $4 \times 0 = 0$ |

**Write an expression for each.**

**1.** a number divided by 6

**2.** a number multiplied by 9

**3.** a number increased by 7

**4.** twelve times a number

**5.** 55 more than a number

**6.** a number divided by 15

**Evaluate. Tell which property you used.**

**7.** $5 \times (20 \times 12)$

**8.** $35 \times 6 \times 0$

**9.** $25 \times 7 \times 4$

**10.** $1 \times 19 \times 2$

**11.** $10 \times 13 \times 10$

**12.** $(9 \times 5) \times 2$

**Evaluate each expression, given $a = 6$, $b = 3$, and $c = 4$.**

**13.** $a \times (b + c)$ _____

**14.** $(a \times b) + c$ _____

## Problem Solving

**Show Your Work**

**15.** Alan and three friends split the cost of a gift. Write an expression that shows how much each person contributed for the gift. Then use the expression to determine how much Alan contributed if the gift cost $48.

Use with text pages 60–61.

Name _____ Date _____

# Model the Distributive Property

| Distributive Property |
|---|

$$a(b + c) = (a \times b) + (a \times c)$$

$$8 \times 24 = 8 \times (20 + 4)$$
$$= (8 \times 20) + (8 \times 4)$$
$$= \quad 160 \quad + \quad 32$$
$$= \quad 192$$

**Use the Distributive Property to multiply. Show the partial products for each and find the sum. Then write a multiplication sentence for each.**

1.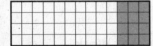

2.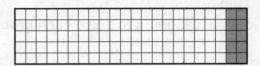

3.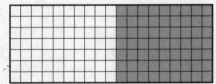

4.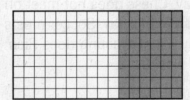

**Draw and divide a rectangle to show each product. Use the Distributive Property to find the product.**

5. $3 \times 17$

6. $6 \times 24$

**Use with text pages 62–63.**

Name _____ Date _____

# Problem-Solving Strategy:
# Use Logical Reasoning

**Ask Yourself**

**Understand**  What facts do I know?

**Plan**  Will a table help me solve the problem?

**Solve**  What questions do I need to ask myself as I use the tables?
Does my table include enough information?

**Look Back**  Does the solution make sense?

**Use logical reasoning to solve each problem.**

**Show Your Work**

1. Rico is a member of a soccer team, a chess club, a school band, and a drama club. Each group meets on a different weekday. Rico has no meetings on Friday. Drama meets the day before soccer. The band does not meet on Thursday. Chess does not meet on Tuesday or Wednesday. Soccer meets on Wednesday. What meeting does Rico have each weekday?

Explain your thinking.

2. Bessie, Liang, Maria, and Seth have one backpack each. Each backpack is a different color. Maria's backpack is not black. Bessie's backpack is not green or blue. Liang's backpack is yellow. Seth's backpack is not green. What color is each person's backpack?

Explain your thinking.

16

**Use with text pages 64–67.**

# Multiply by One-Digit Numbers

**Ways to Multiply by a One-Digit Number**

$$\begin{array}{r} \overset{3}{}\overset{1}{}\phantom{0} \\ 3\,8\,4 \\ \times \phantom{00} 4 \\ \hline 1,5\,3\,6 \end{array}$$

$$\begin{aligned} 4 \times 384 &= 4 \times (300 + 80 + 4) \\ &= (4 \times 300) + (4 \times 80) + (4 \times 4) \\ &= 1,200 + 320 + 16 \longleftarrow \text{partial product} \\ &= 1,536 \end{aligned}$$

**Find the product.**

1. $\begin{array}{r} 95 \\ \times\ 7 \\ \hline \end{array}$
2. $\begin{array}{r} 58 \\ \times\ 6 \\ \hline \end{array}$
3. $\begin{array}{r} 561 \\ \times\ 9 \\ \hline \end{array}$
4. $\begin{array}{r} 737 \\ \times\ 5 \\ \hline \end{array}$

5. $\begin{array}{r} 3,815 \\ \times\ \ \ 4 \\ \hline \end{array}$
6. $\begin{array}{r} 7,462 \\ \times\ \ \ 8 \\ \hline \end{array}$
7. $\begin{array}{r} 16,529 \\ \times\ \ \ \ 3 \\ \hline \end{array}$
8. $\begin{array}{r} 27,832 \\ \times\ \ \ \ 6 \\ \hline \end{array}$

9. $285,115 \times 3$

_____

10. $2 \times 474,691$

_____

**Complete the function table.**

11. **Rule:** $y = 3x$

| x | 218 | 785 | 3,946 | 6,148 | 12,552 |
|---|-----|-----|-------|-------|--------|
| y | _____ | _____ | _____ | _____ | _____ |

**Use the Distributive Property to rewrite each expression. Then solve.**

12. $7 \times 2,393$

13. $52,816 \times 4$

## Problem Solving

14. There are 144 notebooks in one carton. How many notebooks are in 8 cartons?

_____

**Show Your Work**

**Use with text pages 68–71.**

Name _____   Date _____

# Algebra: Mental Math: Patterns in Multiples of 10

---

### Different Ways to Multiply Multiples by 10

Multiply. $7 \times 4,000 = n$

| Use a pattern. | Use mental math. |
|---|---|
| $7 \times 4 = 28$ | $7 \times 4,000 = 7 \times 4 \times 1,000$ |
| $7 \times 40 = 280$ | $= 28 \times 1,000$ |
| $7 \times 400 = 2,800$ | $= 28,000$ |
| $7 \times 4,000 = 28,000$ | |

---

**Use a pattern or mental math to find each product.**

1.  $\begin{array}{r} 70 \\ \times\ 8 \\ \hline \end{array}$
2.  $\begin{array}{r} 600 \\ \times\ 9 \\ \hline \end{array}$
3.  $\begin{array}{r} 4,000 \\ \times\ 7 \\ \hline \end{array}$
4.  $\begin{array}{r} 9,000 \\ \times\ 5 \\ \hline \end{array}$

5.  $\begin{array}{r} 30 \\ \times 80 \\ \hline \end{array}$
6.  $\begin{array}{r} 500 \\ \times 70 \\ \hline \end{array}$
7.  $\begin{array}{r} 900 \\ \times 90 \\ \hline \end{array}$
8.  $\begin{array}{r} 6,000 \\ \times\ 80 \\ \hline \end{array}$

**Multiply.**

9. $37 \times 60$

10. $55 \times 80$

11. $728 \times 30$

12. $641 \times 70$

_____  _____  _____  _____

13. $398 \times 20$

14. $566 \times 50$

15. $813 \times 40$

16. $435 \times 60$

_____  _____  _____  _____

## Problem Solving

**Show Your Work**

17. Ed and his brother are participating in a bike-a-thon for charity. They will each bike 40 miles a day for 15 days. How far will they bike altogether?

_____

**Use with text pages 72–73.**

Name _____    Date _____

# Estimate Products

| Different Ways to Estimate Products | | | | | | |
|---|---|---|---|---|---|---|
| **Front-end Estimation** | | **Rounding** | | **Find a Range** | | |
| 84 | 80 | 84 | 80 | 84 | 80 | 90 |
| ×37 | × 30 | ×37 | × 40 | ×37 | × 30 | × 40 |
| | 2,400 | | 3,200 | | 2,400 | 3,600 |

**Estimate by using front-end estimation. Then estimate by rounding.**

1. 26 × 49     2. 53 × 45     3. 18 × 79     4. 32 × 21

_____     _____     _____     _____

5. 43 × 629     6. 85 × 442     7. 653 × 27     8. 831 × 56

_____     _____     _____     _____

**Estimate. Give a range which includes the actual product. Then find the actual product.**

9. 23 × 79     10. 46 × 33     11. 71 × 19     12. 55 × 42

_____     _____     _____     _____

## Problem Solving

13. Every workday, Mr. Perez drives 134 miles to work and back. About how far does he drive in a month with 19 workdays?

**Show Your Work**

_____

**Use with text pages 74–75.**

# Multiply by Two-Digit Numbers

---

### Different Ways to Multiply Two-Digit Numbers

$$
\begin{array}{r}
\overset{1}{\overset{2}{1}} \\
147 \\
\times\ 24 \\
\hline
588 \\
+\ 2940 \\
\hline
\textbf{3,528}
\end{array}
$$

$$147 \times 24 = 147 \times (20 + 4)$$
$$= (147 \times 20) + (147 \times 4)$$
$$=\quad 2,940\quad +\quad 588$$
$$=\quad \textbf{3,528}$$

---

**Find each product. Estimate or use a calculator to check.**

1.  $\begin{array}{r} 65 \\ \times 29 \\ \hline \end{array}$

2.  $\begin{array}{r} 86 \\ \times 51 \\ \hline \end{array}$

3.  $\begin{array}{r} 75 \\ \times 32 \\ \hline \end{array}$

4.  $\begin{array}{r} 94 \\ \times 17 \\ \hline \end{array}$

5.  $\begin{array}{r} 346 \\ \times\ 27 \\ \hline \end{array}$

6.  $\begin{array}{r} 591 \\ \times\ 54 \\ \hline \end{array}$

7.  $\begin{array}{r} 229 \\ \times\ 65 \\ \hline \end{array}$

8.  $\begin{array}{r} 198 \\ \times\ 22 \\ \hline \end{array}$

**Use the Distributive Property to rewrite each expression. Then solve.**

9. $35 \times 27$

10. $61 \times 19$

11. $214 \times 73$

12. $725 \times 48$

---

## Problem Solving

**Show Your Work**

13. A principal ordered 25 computers for her school. Each computer costs $859. How much did the computers cost?

_____

**Use with text pages 76–79.**

# Problem-Solving Decision:
# Explain Your Solution

**Ask Yourself**

- Can I estimate the answer?
- Is a range of estimates sufficient?
- Do I need an exact answer?

**Solve. Explain your answer.**

**Show Your Work**

1. A school band is holding a concert
to raise money for new uniforms.
Band members sold 480 tickets to
the concert. If the uniforms cost $3,400,
will a ticket price of $7 be enough to
cover the cost? Explain your thinking.

_____

2. A principal ordered 6 buses for a fifth
grade field trip. There are 265 students
and teachers going on the trip. Each
bus holds a maximum of 48 passengers.
Did the principal order enough buses
for the outing? Explain your thinking.

_____

3. Al wants to buy a new video system
that costs $299. He works 14 hours
a week after school. If Al is paid
$6 per hour, will he have enough
money to buy the system after
4 weeks? Explain your thinking.

_____

**Use with text pages 80–81.**

# Estimate Quotients

---

### Estimate with Compatible Numbers

**Estimate.**

**1,759 ÷ 6 = n**     Round the dividend to a multiple of 10 that can be divided easily by 6.     **1,800 ÷ 6 = n**

$$\begin{array}{r} 300 \\ 6\overline{)1,800} \end{array}$$

The estimated quotient is 300.

---

**Estimate the quotient. Tell what numbers you used for the dividend and divisor.**

1. $7\overline{)487}$

2. $5\overline{)408}$

3. $6\overline{)2,371}$

4. $8\overline{)3,297}$

_____

5. $4\overline{)33,203}$

6. $3\overline{)11,955}$

7. $9\overline{)803,486}$

8. $7\overline{)361,912}$

_____

9. $649 \div 8$

10. $2,479 \div 5$

11. $43,054 \div 6$

12. $208,997 \div 3$

_____

## Problem Solving

**Show Your Work**

13. Seth estimated the quotient of 17,475 ÷ 6 as 3,000. What numbers did Seth use for the dividend and divisor to get this quotient? Is Seth's estimate less than or greater than the actual quotient? Tell how you found your answer.

**Use with text pages 86–87.**

# One-Digit Divisors

### Quotients with Remainders

Divide. $315 \div 6 = n$

If the dividend and divisor
are not compatible numbers,
then the quotient will
include a **remainder**.

$$\begin{array}{r} 52 \text{ R3} \\ 6\overline{)315} \\ -30 \\ \hline 15 \\ -12 \\ \hline 3 \end{array}$$

**Check:** $(52 \times 6) + 3$
$312 + 3$
$315$

**Divide.**

1. $4\overline{)138}$      2. $6\overline{)502}$      3. $2\overline{)9,257}$      4. $7\overline{)5,529}$

5. $9\overline{)71,824}$      6. $3\overline{)12,662}$      7. $5\overline{)614,578}$      8. $4\overline{)183,653}$

9. $429 \div 7$      10. $3,191 \div 6$      11. $15,915 \div 8$      12. $228,010 \div 3$

_____      _____      _____      _____

## Equations

The division statement $17 \div 4 = 4$ R1 can be rewritten as $(4 \times 4) + 1 = 17$. Write and solve
a division statement for each equation.

13. $4a + r = 27$      14. $5b + r = 39$      15. $2b + r = 21$      16. $3a + r = 12$

_____      _____      _____      _____

## Problem Solving

**Show Your Work**

17. Mr. Salvi bought 181 protractors to use
with his classes. If he has 5 classes
with 31 students in each, how many
protractors does he have for each class?
Explain your answer.

**Use with text pages 88–89.**

# Problem-Solving Application:
# Use Operations

| | Ask Yourself |
|---|---|
| **Understand** | What is the question? |
| | What do I know? |
| **Plan** | Is the information correct? |
| | Do I have all the information I need? |
| **Solve** | Which operation(s) should I use? |
| | Did I use the operations in the correct order? |
| **Look Back** | Did I check my answer? |

**Use the table for Problems 1–3.**

**Show Your Work**

1. Juan made 16 birdhouses and 12 mailboxes to sell at a fair. He packed them together in cartons of 6. He also made 25 picture frames and 21 signs. Juan packed these together in cartons of 8. How many cartons will he take to the fair?

| Juan's Craft Corner Prices | |
|---|---|
| Birdhouse | $18 |
| Mailbox | $32 |
| Picture Frame | $12 |
| Welcome Sign | $15 |

2. The materials needed to make one picture frame cost Juan $4. How much money will Juan make if he sells all 25 of his picture frames at the fair?

3. Juan sold half of his mailboxes at the fair. If it costs Juan $13 to make one mailbox, how much money did he make at the fair?

**Use with text pages 90–91.**

Name _____ Date _____

# Divisibility

---

### Divisibility Rules

A number is **divisible** by another number when the quotient is a whole number and there is no remainder. Any **factor** of a given number divides into that number with no remainder.

---

**Tell if each number is divisible by 2, 3, 4, 5, 6, 9, or 10.**

**1.** 712      **2.** 810      **3.** 388      **4.** 621      **5.** 524

_____   _____   _____   _____   _____

**6.** 460      **7.** 1,912      **8.** 5,700      **9.** 3,126      **10.** 1,890

_____   _____   _____   _____   _____

**Use the table for Problems 11–12.**

**11.** Yuri and other members of his class gathered a total number of cans that is divisible by 4. What grade is Yuri in?

_____

**12.** The cans from each grade are packed individually in boxes of 9. Which two grades' cans will have boxes that are partially full?

_____

| Canned Food Drive Totals | |
|---|---|
| **Grade** | **Cans Collected** |
| 3 | 668 |
| 4 | 670 |
| 5 | 702 |
| 6 | 585 |

## Problem Solving

**Show Your Work**

**13.** Conor said that a number divisible by 3 and by 9 is also divisible by 6. Do you agree with Conor? Tell why or why not.

_____

_____

25

**Use with text pages 92–95.**

# Zeros in the Quotient

**Quotients with Zeros**

Divide. $1,421 \div 7 = n$

Sometimes you cannot divide after bringing down a digit from the dividend. You must put a zero in the quotient before bringing down the next digit.

$$\begin{array}{r} 203 \\ 7\overline{)1,421} \\ -14 \phantom{00} \\ \hline 021 \\ -21 \\ \hline 0 \end{array}$$

Multiply. $3 \times 7$
Subtract. $21 - 21$
There is no remainder.

**Check:**

$$\begin{array}{r} 203 \\ \times \phantom{0}7 \\ \hline 1,421 \end{array}$$

**Divide.**

1. $8\overline{)816}$

2. $3\overline{)912}$

3. $5\overline{)547}$

4. $2\overline{)6,016}$

5. $9\overline{)3,655}$

6. $7\overline{)56,765}$

7. $6\overline{)24,425}$

8. $9\overline{)639,045}$

9. $284 \div 7$

10. $4,555 \div 9$

11. $40,723 \div 8$

12. $534,042 \div 6$

## Problem Solving

**Show Your Work**

13. A school band raised $257 in a bake sale and $695 in a patron drive. The band will use this money to buy new hats for the band members. If each hat costs $9, how many hats can the band purchase?

**Use with text pages 96–97.**

# Problem-Solving Strategy:
# Guess and Check

**Ask Yourself**

| | |
|---|---|
| **Understand** | What is the question? |
| | What facts do I know? |
| **Plan** | Can I use Guess and Check to solve the problem? |
| | Did I make a reasonable first guess? |
| **Solve** | Did I check to see whether my guess is correct? |
| | Did I use the results from the first guess to make a better guess? |
| | Can I organize my guesses into a table? |
| **Look Back** | Is my answer reasonable? |
| | Did I solve the problem? |

**Use the Ask Yourself questions to help you
solve each problem.**

1. Rosa has 120 red, white, and blue beads.
She has three times more red beads than
white beads. She has twice as many blue
beads as white beads. How many of each
kind of bead does Rosa have? Organize
your guesses into a table. Did this help
you solve the problem? Explain.

**Show Your Work**

2. Janell spent $40 for an outfit. She paid
for the items using $10, $5, and $1 bills.
If she gave the clerk 10 bills in all, how
many of each bill did she use? Organize
your guesses into a table. Did this help
you solve the problem? Explain.

**Use with text pages 98–100.**

Name _____  Date _____

# Mental Math: Solve Equations

---

### Solving Equations

**Solve** $5n = 40$

Think: What number times 5 equals 40?

$5 \times 8 = 40$

$n = 8$

**Solve** $54 \div n = 9$

Think: 54 divided by what number equals 9?

$54 \div 6 = 9$

$n = 6$

**Solve** $n \div 8 = 6$

Think: What number divided by 8 equals 6?

$48 \div 8 = 6$

$n = 48$

---

**Solve each problem.**

1. Sue worked for 6 hours. She earned $42. How much does Sue earn per hour?

   $6n = 42$

   _____

2. Betty will be able to give each of her seven friends four fruit snacks. How many fruit snacks does she have?

   $n \div 7 = 4$

   _____

**Use mental math to solve the equations.**

3. $32 \div r = 4$     4. $5p = 20$     5. $n \div 7 = 3$     6. $9b = 63$

7. $s \div 6 = 6$     8. $24 \div m = 3$     9. $6t = 18$     10. $5c = 35$

**Replace $n$ with 8. Is the equation true? Write *yes* or *no*.**

11. $45 \div n = 5$     12. $7n = 56$     13. $n \div 1 = n$     14. $n \times n = 16$

## Problem Solving

**Show Your Work**

15. Ali read $n$ pages of her book each day. She finished the 48-page book in 6 days. How many pages did Ali read each day?

   _____

**Use with text pages 102–105.**

# Division with Greater Numbers

**Find 15,286 ÷ 37.**

$$\begin{array}{r} 4 \\ 37\overline{)15{,}286} \\ -14\,8 \\ \hline 4 \end{array}$$

$$\begin{array}{r} 41 \\ 37\overline{)15{,}286} \\ -14\,8 \\ \hline 48 \\ -37 \\ \hline 11 \end{array}$$

$$\begin{array}{r} 413 \textbf{ R5} \\ 37\overline{)15{,}286} \\ -14\,8 \\ \hline 48 \\ -37 \\ \hline 116 \\ -111 \\ \hline 5 \end{array}$$

**Check:** $(413 \times 37) + 5 = 15{,}286$
$15{,}281 + 5 = 15{,}286$
$15{,}286 = 15{,}286$

**Divide. Check your answer.**

1. $56\overline{)2{,}765}$

2. $47\overline{)8{,}795}$

3. $23\overline{)9{,}823}$

4. $16\overline{)91{,}265}$

5. $42\overline{)35{,}874}$

6. $30\overline{)23{,}498}$

7. $225\overline{)78{,}095}$

8. $142\overline{)59{,}336}$

9. $5{,}682 \div 39$

10. $6{,}058 \div 24$

11. $45{,}720 \div 34$

12. $315{,}988 \div 89$

_____   _____   _____   _____

## Problem Solving

13. A local farm has 57 rows of soybean plants. If there are a total of 14,250 soybean plants, how many are in each row?

**Show Your Work**

_____

**Use with text pages 120–123.**

# Algebra: Order of Operations

| Order of Operations | |
|---|---|
| **1.** Simplify the terms within **parentheses**. | $(8 + 5) \times 2^3 - 3$ |
| **2.** Simplify the terms with **exponents**. | $13 \times 2^3 - 3$ |
| **3.** **Multiply** and **divide** from left to right. | $13 \times 8 - 3$ |
| **4.** **Add** and **subtract** from left to right. | $104 - 3 = 101$ |

**Remember: Please excuse my dear Aunt Sally (PEMDAS).**

**Simplify.**

**1.** $(85 - 22) + 4^2$

**2.** $7 + (42 \div 6) \times 5$

**3.** $(55 - 14) + (18 \div 9)^2$

_____

_____

_____

**4.** $(51 \div 3) + (21 \div 7)$

**5.** $1,535 - (34 - 18) \times 4$

**6.** $92 - (58 - 14) + 13$

_____

_____

_____

**7.** $12^2 - (8 \times 7) + 5$

**8.** $(121 \div 11) + 5^2$

**9.** $257 + (3^2 \times 5) - 18$

_____

_____

_____

**Write $>$, $<$, or $=$ for each $\bigcirc$.**

**10.** $43 + (17 - 6) \bigcirc (43 + 17) - 6$

**11.** $(94 - 36) + 41 \bigcirc 94 - (36 + 41)$

**12.** $(5 \times 2^2) + 12 \bigcirc 5 \times (2^2 + 12)$

**13.** $(81 \div 9) \times 3 \bigcirc (81 \div 3) \times 1$

**Evaluate the expressions given $x = 3$ and $y = 5$.**

**14.** $4(x + y) - y^2 =$ _____

**15.** $(x^2 + y^2) - 20 =$ _____

**16.** $(2x + 3y) - y =$ _____

## Problem Solving

**Show Your Work**

**17.** When Anna simplified the expression
$7 \times 9 - 6 \times 4$, she said the result is 228.
Do you agree with Anna? Explain.

**Use with text pages 124–127.**

# Problem-Solving Application:
# Interpret Remainders

When you solve a problem with a remainder, you need to decide how to interpret the remainder.

**Ask Yourself**

**Understand**  What is the question?
What facts do I know?

**Plan**  What operation will I use?
How will I interpret the remainder?

**Solve**  Should the remainder be in the answer or should it be dropped?

**Look Back**  Did I interpret the remainder correctly so that the answer makes sense?

Solve. Explain how you decided to interpret each remainder.

**Show Your Work**

1. There are 295 students and teachers going on a field trip. Each bus holds 48 people. How many buses are needed for the trip?

_____

2. Guides took groups of 48 on a nature hike. Each guide led two different hikes. How many guides were needed for the 295 students and teachers?

_____

3. During the trip, the students and teachers drank 894 juice packs. The packs came in cartons of 24. How many cartons were opened during the trip?

_____

**Use with text pages 128–131.**

# Measurement Concepts

> ## Units of Measure
>
> The smaller the unit of measure you use, the more **precise** the measure.
>
> The segment is:
>
> inches  1    2    3    4
>
> • 3 inches long when measured to the nearest inch.
> • $2\frac{3}{4}$ inches long when measured to the nearest quarter inch.

**Estimate the length of each object. Then use a tape measure, yardstick, or ruler to measure each object.**

|   | | Estimate | Actual |
|---|---|---|---|
| 1. | the width of this paper | _____ | _____ |
| 2. | the length of your ring finger | _____ | _____ |
| 3. | the width of the classroom door | _____ | _____ |
| 4. | the length of a key | _____ | _____ |
| 5. | the length of your leg from heel to knee | _____ | _____ |

**Tell whether a measurement is needed or if an estimate is sufficient. Explain your answer.**

6. You need to find the width of a piano to see if it will fit through a doorway.     _____

7. You need to know the distance from your house to school to see about how far you travel each day.     _____

## Problem Solving

**Show Your Work**

8. If you were having your feet measured for shoes, would you need to have a precise measure? Would a quarter inch short make a big difference? Explain.

_____

**Use with text pages 148–149.**

# Customary Units of Length

| | How many feet are in 288 inches? | How many feet are in 4 yards 2 feet? |
|---|---|---|
| 12 inches (in.) = 1 foot (ft) | Remember: Divide to change from a smaller to a larger unit. | Remember: Multiply to change from a larger to a smaller unit. |
| 3 feet = 1 yard (yd) | 288 in. = ☐ ft | 4 yd 2 ft = ☐ ft |
| 36 inches = 1 yard | $288 \div 12 = 24$ | $4 \times 3 = 12$ |
| 5,280 feet = 1 mile (mi) | 288 in. = 24 ft | 12 ft + 2 ft = 14 ft |
| 1,760 yards = 1 mile | | |

**Complete.**

**1.** ____ ft = 6 yd     **2.** 3 mi = ____ ft     **3.** 24 yd = ____ ft

**4.** 114 in. = ____ ft ____ in.   **5.** 8,000 ft = ____ mi ____ ft   **6.** 180 in. = ____ ft

**Compare. Write >, <, or = for each ○.**

**7.** 6 ft ○ 72 in.     **8.** 150 in. ○ 5 yd     **9.** 2 mi ○ 10,000 ft

**Which unit would you use to measure each? Write *inch*, *foot*, *yard*, or *mile*.**

**10.** the length of a puppy _____     **11.** the length of a soccer field _____

**12.** the width of your state _____     **13.** the height of a van _____

## Problem Solving

**Show Your Work**

**14.** Gayle has 5 yd 2 ft of wire. Mae has 204 in. of wire. Who has more wire? Explain how you found your answer.

**Use with text pages 150–151.**

# Customary Units of Weight and Capacity

| Customary Units of Weight | Customary Units of Capacity |
|---|---|
| 16 ounces (oz) = 1 pound (lb) | 8 fluid ounces (fl oz) = 1 cup (c) |
| 2,000 pounds = 1 ton (T) | 2 cups = 1 pint (pt) |
| | 16 fluid ounces = 1 pint |
| | 2 pints = 1 quart (qt) |
| | 4 quarts = 1 gallon (gal) |

**Complete.**

**1.** 15 pt = ____ qt ____ pt   **2.** 30 qt = ____ gal ____ qt   **3.** 14 c = ____ pt

**4.** 72 oz = ____ lb ____ oz   **5.** 13,200 T = ____ T ____ lb   **6.** ____ pt = 12 qt

**Compare. Write >, <, or = for each ◯.**

**7.** 100 oz ◯ 6 lb          **8.** 5 T ◯ 10,000 lb          **9.** 9 c ◯ 5 pt

**Which unit would you use to measure each? Write *oz, lb, T, fl oz, c, pt, qt,* or *gal.***

**10.** Capacity of a bathtub _____          **11.** Weight of a truck _____

**12.** Your weight _____          **13.** Capacity of a juice box _____

## Problem Solving

**Show Your Work**

**14.** Jake needs 25 cups of apple juice for a class party. How many quarts of juice should he buy?

_____

**Use with text pages 152–155.**

# Metric Units of Length

| Metric Units of Length | Changing Metric Units of Length | |
|---|---|---|
| 10 millimeters (mm) = 1 centimeter (cm) | Multiply to change from a larger to a smaller unit. | Divide to change from a smaller to a larger unit. |
| 10 centimeters = 1 decimeter (dm) | 4 km = ☐ m | 500 mm = ☐ cm |
| 10 decimeters = 1 meter (m) | 4 × 1,000 = 4,000 | 500 ÷ 10 = 50 |
| 1,000 meters = 1 kilometer (km) | 4 km = 4,000 m | 500 mm = 50 cm |

**Use a ruler. Measure each line segment in decimeters, centimeters, and millimeters.**

1. •——————————————————————•

_____

2. •————————————————————————————•

_____

3. •————————————————————•

_____

4. •——————————————————————•

_____

**Complete.**

**5.** 55 m = ____ dm      **6.** ____ cm = 20 mm      **7.** 9 m = ____ cm

**Compare. Write >, <, or = for each ◯.**

**8.** 50 cm ◯ 5 dm      **9.** 8 km ◯ 9,000 m      **10.** 200 dm ◯ 2 m

## Problem Solving

**Show Your Work**

**11.** Name a distance you would measure in kilometers and a distance you would measure in meters.

**Use with text pages 156–159.**

# Metric Units of Mass and Capacity

| **Metric Units of Mass** | **Metric Units of Capacity** |
|---|---|
| 1,000 milligrams (mg) = 1 gram (g) | 1,000 milliliters (mL) = 1 liter (L) |
| 1,000 grams = 1 kilogram (kg) | 10 deciliters (dL) = 1 liter (L) |
| 1,000 kilograms = 1 metric ton (t) | |

**Complete.**

1. 8 L = ____ dL

2. ____ t = 6,000 kg

3. 9 g = ____ mg

4. ____ L = 50,000 mL

5. 8 kg = ____ g

6. 20 t = ____ kg

**Compare. Write >, <, or = for each ○.**

7. 16 dL ○ 160 L

8. 7 kg ○ 700 g

9. 13 t ○ 13,000 kg

**Tell which metric unit you would choose to measure each. Explain your choice.**

10. amount of juice in a large pitcher _____

11. mass of a car _____

12. mass of a box of cereal _____

13. amount of honey on a spoon _____

## Problem Solving

**Show Your Work**

14. The mass of Box A is 3 kg. The mass of
Box B is 2 kg 550 g. The mass of Box C
is 3,500 g. How would you list the boxes
from least to greatest mass? Tell how
you found your answer.

**Use with text pages 160–163.**

# Add and Subtract Measurements

**Ask Yourself**

- Are the units the same?

- Do I need to regroup or simplify?

$2\ g - 400\ mg = 2{,}000\ mg - 400\ mg = 1{,}600\ mg$

$8\ ft\ 3\ in. + 2\ ft\ 10\ in. = 10\ ft\ 13\ in. = 11\ ft\ 1\ in.$

**Add or subtract.**

1.    6 L 8 dL
      + 9 L 7 dL

2.    8 yd 1 ft
      − 3 yd 2 ft

3.    5 T 1800 lb
      + 1 T  550 lb

4.    7 h 15 min
      − 2 h 40 min

5.    3 g 800 mg
      + 9 g 700 mg

6.    14 m 1 dm
      − 8 m 9 dm

7.  2 gal − 3 pt

8.  4 yd − 2 ft 3 in.

9.  9 lb 10 oz + 2 lb 12 oz

**Find the length represented by $z$.**

10.  $6\ yd - z = 2\ yd\ 3\ ft$

11.  $z - 2\ km = 1\ km\ 700\ m$

12.  $3\ ft - z = 9\ in.$

## Problem Solving

**Show Your Work**

13. Mina poured 8 fl oz of juice concentrate into a 2 quart pitcher. How much water should she add to fill the pitcher? Tell how you found your answer.

**Use with text pages 164–165.**

# Problem-Solving Decisions:
# Multistep Problems

| | | Ask Yourself | |
|---|---|---|---|
| **Understand** | What is the question? | | |
| | What data do I need to use to solve the problem? | | |
| **Plan** | Which operation or operations do I need to use to solve the problem? | | |
| **Solve** | Did I do the operations in the correct order? | | |
| **Look Back** | Did I answer the question? | | |
| | Does my answer make sense? | | |

**Use the schedule to solve. Show all your steps.**

| Station | Bus 115 | Bus 228 | Bus 317 |
|---|---|---|---|
| Mount Holly | 7:15 A.M. | 8:38 A.M. | 7:45 A.M. |
| Springfield | 7:28 A.M. | – – – – | 7:58 A.M. |
| Millerville | – – – – | 9:02 A.M. | 8:25 A.M. |
| Oceanside | 8:37 A.M. | 9:42 A.M. | 9:05 A.M. |

**Show Your Work**

1. Tom and Leon both travel from Springfield to Oceanside. Tom takes Bus 115 while Leon takes Bus 317. Whose trip takes more time? How much more?

   _____

   _____

2. Deb, Sarah, and Jane all live in Mount Holly and work in Oceanside. Deb takes Bus 228, Sarah takes Bus 317, and Jane takes Bus 115. How would you list the females from shortest to longest trip?

   _____

   _____

42

**Use with text pages 166–167.**

# Double Bar Graphs

---

**Steps to Making a Double Bar Graph**

**Step 1:** Draw the axes.

**Step 2:** Choose an appropriate scale and mark equal intervals.

**Step 3:** Label the horizontal axis with the information the bars show.

**Step 4:** Draw the bars.

**Step 5:** Make a key to help observers read the graph. Give the graph a title.

---

**Use the graph for Problems 1–7.**

1. How many students have Golden Retrievers?

   _____

2. What is the difference in the number of fifth- and sixth-graders who own Siberian Huskies?

   _____

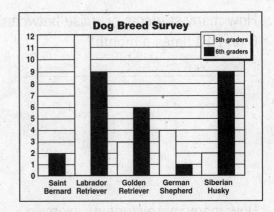

3. How many fifth-grade students own either a Labrador Retriever or a German Shepherd?

   _____

4. What two breeds are owned by a total of 16 fifth-grade students?

   _____

5. What breed has a total equal to the number of sixth-grade students who own a Siberian Husky?

   _____

6. Why was only one bar drawn above the label *Saint Bernard?*

   _____

---

## Problem Solving

7. How many students participated in the survey? Explain how you found your answer.

**Show Your Work**

43

**Use with text pages 172–175.**

# Histograms

---

**Steps to Making a Histogram**

**Step 1:** Give the graph a title.

**Step 2:** Draw the axes. Label the vertical axis. Choose an appropriate scale and mark equal intervals.

**Step 3:** Label the horizontal axis with the information the bars show.

**Step 4:** Draw the bars. Do not leave spaces between the bars.

---

**Use the graph for Problems 1–8.**

1. How many students exercise between 6 and 10 times a month?

   _____

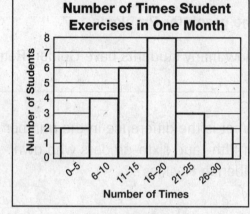

2. How many more students exercise between 16 and 20 times a month than between 26 and 30 times a month?

   _____

3. How many students exercise 10 or fewer times a month?

   _____

4. How many students exercise more than 20 times a month?

   _____

5. What three intervals have a total equal to the number of students who exercise between 16 and 20 times a month?

   _____

6. How many students were surveyed?

   _____

7. How would you list the intervals from least to greatest number of students?

   _____

---

**Problem Solving**

8. Why does the histogram end with a maximum of 30 times a month?

   _____

**Show Your Work**

**Use with text pages 176–177.**

Name _____ Date _____

# Line and Double Line Graphs

---

**Steps to Making a Line Graph**

**Step 1:** Draw the axes. Label the horizontal axis. Choose an appropriate scale and mark equal intervals.

**Step 2:** Label the horizontal axis with the information it shows.

**Step 3:** Plot the ordered pairs. Connect the points with a straight line.

**Step 4:** Give the graph a title.

---

**Use the graph for Problems 1–6.**

1. How many gallons of apple juice were sold at 12:00?

_____

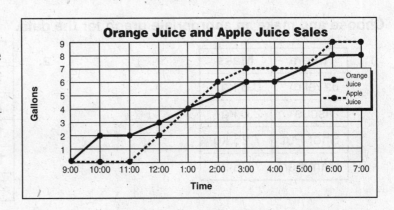

2. At what times were orange juice and apple juice sales equal?

_____

3. Between 9:00 and 11:00, how many more gallons of orange juice were sold than apple juice?

_____

4. How many gallons of apple juice were sold between 1:01 PM and 4:00 PM?

_____

5. What pattern occurs in the amount of apple juice sold between 11:00 and 2:00?

_____

---

## Problem Solving

6. How many gallons of juice were sold between 9:00 and 7:00? Tell how you found your answer.

_____

**Show Your Work**

45

**Use with text pages 178–181.**

# Choose an Appropriate Graph

---

### Different Types of Graphs

A **bar graph** is appropriate when the data can be counted and you want to make comparisons.

A **line graph** is appropriate when you want to show change over time.

A **pictograph** is a good choice when the data are multiples of a number.

A **circle graph** is a good choice when the data are parts of a whole.

A **histogram** is a good choice to show how frequently data occur within equal intervals.

---

**Choose and make an appropriate graph for the data.**

**1.**

| Event | Mass |
|---|---|
| Javelin | 0.8 kg |
| Discus | 2.0 kg |
| Shot Put | 7.26 kg |
| Hammer | 7.26 kg |

**2.**

| Time | Number of Students |
|---|---|
| 10–12 sec | 3 |
| 13–15 sec | 5 |
| 16–18 sec | 10 |
| 19–21 sec | 6 |
| 22–24 sec | 2 |

**3.**

| Event | Record |
|---|---|
| Javelin, women's | 74.68 m |
| Javelin, men's | 89.66 m |
| Discus, women's | 72.30 m |
| Discus, men's | 68.82 m |
| Shotput, women's | 22.41 m |
| Shotput, men's | 22.47 m |

**4.**

| Sport | Number of Students |
|---|---|
| Baseball | 16 |
| Football | 8 |
| Soccer | 12 |
| Softball | 4 |
| Hockey | 4 |
| Total | 44 |

---

## Problem Solving

**5.** If you wanted to make a pictograph for the data set in Problem 4, how many students should each picture represent? Explain why.

**Show Your Work**

---

**Use with text pages 182–183.**

# Misleading Graphs

| Misleading Graphs |
|---|
| A **misleading graph** shows data in a false, or misleading, way.<br><br>To see if a graph is misleading, ask yourself:<br><br>• Does the graph have a zigzag line to show that numbers are missing from the scale?<br><br>• Does the graph have a scale with equal intervals? |

1. The two graphs show the same information. Which graph seems misleading? Explain.

_____

**Use the smaller graph for Problems 2–3.**

2. Tell why it seems that more than four times more visitors came to the Science Fair on Sunday than on thursday.

_____

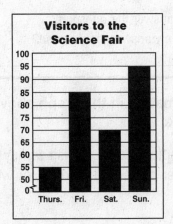

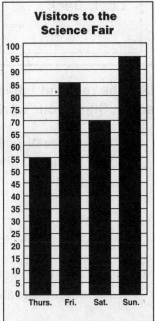

3. How many more visitors went to the fair on Saturday than on Thursday? How many more went on Sunday than on Friday? Do the bars accurately show these differences? Tell why or why not.

_____

## Problem Solving

4. Change the intervals of the misleading graph above from 5 to 50. Would this affect the appearance of the graph? Is the graph still misleading? Explain your answer.

_____

**Show Your Work**

**Use with text pages 184–185.**

# Problem-Solving Decisions: Relevant Information

**Use the relevant information in the graph above to solve. Show your work.**

**Reasons Why People Are Flying**

1. The number of people who fly to visit family is equal to the number of people who fly for what two reasons?

   _____

   _____

2. How would you list the reasons why people fly from least to greatest?

   _____

   _____

   _____

3. How many people participated in the survey? Tell how you found your answer.

   _____

   _____

**Use with text pages 186–187.**

# Collect and Organize Data

**Steps to Making a Survey**

**Step 1:** Decide on a survey question.

**Step 2:** List five or six answer choices for the question on a recording sheet.

**Step 3:** Pose the survey question to group of people. Use a tally mark to record each answer.

**Step 4:** Count the tally marks for each answer. Record the total in the Frequency column.

**Step 5:** Analyze the results.

**The table shows the results of a survey of a fifth-grade class. Use the Data Table for Problems 1–6.**

1. Complete the Frequency column of the table.

2. How many of those surveyed have read exactly two books?

   _____

3. Which answer choices received an equal number of votes? How many votes did each receive?

   _____

| Number of Books Read | Tally | Frequency |
|---|---|---|
| 1 | ||| | |
| 2 | ||||| | | |
| 3 | ||||| ||| | |
| 4 | |||| | |
| 5 | || | |
| More than 5 | ||| | |

4. How many people responded to the survey?

   _____

5. How many more people gave the most popular answer choice than the least popular answer choice?

   _____

## Problem Solving

**Show Your Work**

6. Would the results of this survey be different if the question were asked of children between the ages of 3 and 5? Tell why or why not.

   _____

   _____

**Use with text pages 192–193.**

# Mean, Median, Mode, and Range

| | |
|---|---|
| **Mean** | Sum of the numbers divided by the number of addends |
| **Median** | Middle number when data is arranged in order |
| **Mode** | Number that occurs most often |
| **Range** | Difference between the greatest and least values |
| **Cluster** | Several data points in a small interval |
| **Gap** | A large space between data |

**Make a Line Plot to Organize Data**

**Step 1:** List the data in order.

**Step 2:** Make a number line that covers the range of numbers in your list.

**Step 3:** Put an X above each number as many times as that number appears in the list.

**Make a line plot for each set of data. Identify clusters and gaps. Then find the mean, median, mode, and range.**

1. time in seconds
   65, 57, 63, 60, 63, 65, 59, 61, 65

   Mean _____

   Median _____

   Mode _____

   Range _____

2. ages in years
   4, 14, 29, 24, 20, 42, 21, 30, 14

   Mean _____

   Median _____

   Mode _____

   Range _____

**Find the mean, median, and mode for each set of data.**

3. 25, 83, 30, 84, 42, 87, 73, 69, 83

   Mean _____

   Median _____

   Mode _____

4. 106, 98, 114, 111, 105, 98, 110

   Mean _____

   Median _____

   Mode _____

5. 77, 75, 71, 82, 85, 89, 80, 72, 71

   Mean _____

   Median _____

   Mode _____

## Problem Solving

**Show Your Work**

6. Dixie claims to be able to determine the mode of data by simply looking at a line plot. Do you think this is possible? Tell why or why not?

   _____

**Use with text pages 194–197.**

# Make and Use a Stem-and-Leaf Plot

| Steps to Making a Stem-and-Leaf Plot | | Number of Amusement Parks in Different Countries | |
|---|---|---|---|
| | | **Stem** | **Leaf** |
| **Step 1:** Write a title. | | 0 | 2 2 3 4 4 4 5 6 7 |
| **Step 2:** Write the tens digits needed to represent the data in order from least to greatest. Each of these numbers is a **stem**. | | 1 | 1 1 1 3 4 5 8 |
| | | 2 | |
| **Step 3:** For each piece of data, write the ones digit, or **leaf**, next to its tens digit. Arrange the digits from least to greatest. | | 3 | 8 |
| | | 4 | 7 |
| | | 5 | |
| | | 6 | |
| 7|4 means 74. | | 7 | 4 |

**Use the stem-and-leaf plot for Problems 1–5.**

| | Number of Birds Observed by Each Group | |
|---|---|---|
| | **Stem** | **Leaf** |
| | 0 | 2 4 |
| | 1 | 2 5 6 9 |
| | 2 | 2 3 5 7 9 9 9 |
| 0|2 means 2. | 3 | 1 3 |

**1.** What does 1|2 mean?

_____

**2.** How many groups observed fewer than 20 birds?

_____

**3.** How many groups are represented in the data?

_____

**4.** How many groups observed 25 or more birds?

_____

**5.** What is the mean, median, mode, and range of this data?

_____

## Problem Solving

**6.** On the back of this paper, make a stem-and-leaf plot for this set of data: 12, 38, 26, 8, 9, 14, 27, 26, 11, 4, 24, 36. Explain how you can use your completed stem-and-leaf plot to find the mode of the data.

_____

**Show Your Work**

**Use with text pages 198–199.**

# Problem Solving Strategy:
# Make a Table

**Ask Yourself**

| | |
|---|---|
| **Understand** | What facts do I know? |
| **Plan** | Did I make a table with the correct headings and ranges? |
| **Solve** | Did I tally the table? |
| | Did I find the frequency for each range? |
| **Look Back** | Did I check my answer? |

**Make a table to solve each problem.**

**Make your table here.**

1. Marcus asked his classmates how many hours they spend doing homework each week. His set of data is shown below.

   5, 6, 8, 10, 7, 6, 8, 2, 7, 11, 9, 6,
   3, 5, 14, 8, 9, 10, 4, 5, 7, 8, 12, 10

   Do most of his classmates spend between 1 and 5 hours, between 6 and 10 hours, or between 11 and 15 hours on homework each week?

   _____

2. Dave recorded the ages of the first twenty people to enter a movie theater. His set of data is shown below.

   32, 18, 21, 25, 28, 15, 47, 55, 51, 29
   17, 19, 26, 22, 38, 61, 57, 35, 44, 33

   Were more of the people between the ages of 1 and 10, or 11 and 20, or 21 and 30, or 31 and 40, or 41 and 50, or 51 and 60, or 61 and higher?

   _____

52

**Use with text pages 200–203.**

# Draw Conclusions and Make Predictions

**Use the data from the line plot for Problems 1–3.**

1. How many holes were played?

   _____

2. Find the mean, median, and mode of the data.

   Mean _____

   Median _____

   Mode _____

3. Use the mean, median, or mode to predict how many strokes you would need to complete a golf hole. Explain your answer.

   _____

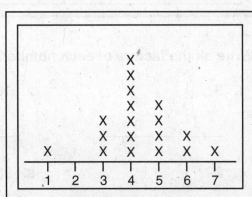

**Number of Strokes to Complete Golf Hole**

**Use the data from the table for Problems 4–7.**

4. Show the data on a line plot.

| Runs Scored by Tigers Baseball Team |
| --- |
| 9 6 2 8 7 3 5 1 4 6 2 6 5 7 4 |

5. What is the mean and median of the data?

   Mean _____

   Median _____

6. What is the mode and range of the data?

   Mode _____

   Range _____

## Problem Solving

7. Suppose you were the coach of the next team the Tigers face. How many runs do you think your team needs to score in order to beat the Tigers? Give reasons for your answer.

   _____

**Show Your Work**

**Use with text pages 204–207.**

# Prime and Composite Numbers

> **Find the factors of 50**
>
> - $50 \div 1 = 50$     Begin by trying to divide 50 by each number starting with 1.
> - $50 \div 2 = 25$     Stop when a factor is repeated.
> - $50 \div 5 = 10$
>
> The factors of 50 are 1, 2, 5, 10, 25, and 50.
> It is a composite number.

**Write all the factors of each number. Then identify the number as *prime* or *composite*.**

1. 9

2. 16

3. 20

4. 29

5. 33

6. 37

7. 42

8. 45

9. 49

10. 51

11. 68

12. 99

## Problem Solving

13. Scott has 72 baseball cards. He wants to display them in rows with an equal number of cards. How many different ways can Scott set up the rows?

**Show Your Work**

**Use with text pages 224–225.**

# Prime Factorization

| **Write the prime factorization of 24.** | | |
|---|---|---|
| **Step 1:** Write 24 as the product of 2 factors. | **Step 2:** Write the factors of each composite factor. | **Step 3:** Write the prime factors. |
|  24 / \ 4 × 6 |  24 / \ 4 × 6 / \ / \ 2×2 2×3 | $24 = 2 \times 2 \times 2 \times 3$ $24 = 2^3 \times 3$ |

**Complete the factor tree. Then write the prime factorization.**

1. 20
   2 × □
   2 × 2 × □
   $2^{□}$ × □

2.  20
   4 × □
   □ × 2 × □
   $□^{2}$ × □

**Write the prime factorization of each number. Use exponents if possible. If the number is prime, write _prime_.**

3. 28

_____

4. 23

_____

5. 30

_____

6. 42

_____

7. 65

_____

8. 56

_____

9. 100

_____

10. 81

_____

11. 41

_____

## Problem Solving

**Show Your Work**

12. Name two numbers whose prime factor-ization includes the numbers 2, 3, and 5. Write the prime factorization of each.

_____

Use with text pages 226–227.

# Greatest Common Factor

| Different Ways to Find the GCF of 15 and 20 | | |
|---|---|---|
| **Way 1:** Make a list. | | **Way 2:** Use prime factorization. |
| 15: 1, 3, **5**, 15 | The GCF is 5. | $15 = 3 \times 5$ |
| 20: 1, 2, 4, **5**, 10, 20 | | $20 = 2^2 \times 5$ |

**List the factors of each number. Then find the greatest common factor of the numbers.**

**1.** 16, 42

_____

**2.** 21, 25

_____

**3.** 24, 56

_____

**4.** 12, 30

_____

**Write the prime factorization using exponents of each number. Then find the greatest common factor (GCF) of the numbers.**

**5.** 24, 36

_____

**6.** 21, 56

_____

**7.** 45, 81

_____

**8.** 50, 75

_____

## Problem Solving

**Show Your Work**

**9.** Tia made 50 cupcakes and 160 cookies for a bake sale. She put the items in packages with an equal number of cupcakes and cookies. How many packages did she make? What was in each package?

_____

**Use with text pages 228–231.**

# Least Common Multiple

| Different Ways to Find the LCM of 8 and 20 | | |
|---|---|---|
| **Way 1:** Make a list. | | **Way 2:** Use prime factorization. |
| 8: 8, 16, 24, 32, **40**, 48 | The LCM is 40. | $8 = 2^3$ |
| 20: 20, **40**, 60, 80, 100 | | $20 = \mathbf{2^2 \times 5}$ |

**Write the first five multiples of each number.**

**1.** 9

**2.** 13

**3.** 15

_____

_____

_____

**4.** 21

**5.** 19

**6.** 50

_____

_____

_____

**Write the prime factorization of each number.**

**7.** 14

**8.** 18

**9.** 48

_____

_____

_____

**Find the LCM of the numbers in each pair. Use either method.**

**10.** 15, 18

**11.** 12, 32

**12.** 15, 45

_____

_____

_____

**13.** 24, 40

**14.** 36, 72

**15.** 28, 42

_____

_____

_____

## Problem Solving

**Show Your Work**

**16.** Stacey jogs every third day and swims
every fourth day. If she is jogging on
Monday, what day of the week will
she end up jogging and swimming?

_____

**Use with text pages 232–235.**

Name _____  Date _____

# Fractions and Mixed Numbers

| Improper Fractions and Mixed Numbers | |
|---|---|
| Divide to change an improper fraction to a mixed number. | Multiply and add to change a mixed number to an improper fraction. |
| $\begin{array}{r} 2 \\ 4\overline{)9} \\ -8 \\ \hline 1 \end{array}$  So, $\frac{9}{4} = 2\frac{1}{4}$ | $2\frac{1}{4} = \frac{(4 \times 2) + 1}{4} = \frac{9}{4}$  So, $\frac{9}{4} = 2\frac{1}{4}$ |

**Study this number line. Write each missing fraction. Then draw a different model to represent each fraction you wrote.**

1. 
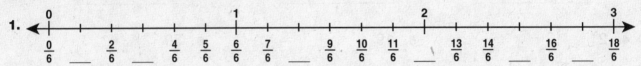

$\frac{0}{6}$ ___ $\frac{2}{6}$ ___ $\frac{4}{6}$ $\frac{5}{6}$ $\frac{6}{6}$ $\frac{7}{6}$ ___ $\frac{9}{6}$ $\frac{10}{6}$ $\frac{11}{6}$ ___ $\frac{13}{6}$ $\frac{14}{6}$ ___ $\frac{16}{6}$ ___ $\frac{18}{6}$

_____

**Write each improper fraction as a mixed number or a whole number.**

2. $\frac{15}{4}$ 

3. $\frac{19}{5}$ 

4. $\frac{21}{7}$ 

5. $\frac{20}{9}$

6. $\frac{11}{3}$ 

7. $\frac{26}{2}$ 

8. $\frac{31}{5}$ 

9. $\frac{21}{8}$

**Write each mixed number as an improper fraction.**

10. $1\frac{4}{5}$ 

11. $3\frac{1}{3}$ 

12. $5\frac{5}{6}$ 

13. $2\frac{7}{8}$

14. $4\frac{1}{2}$ 

15. $7\frac{3}{4}$ 

16. $1\frac{9}{10}$ 

17. $2\frac{7}{9}$

## Problem Solving

**Show Your Work**

18. A whole pizza has 8 slices. Tina has $3\frac{5}{8}$ pizzas. How many slices does she have?

_____

**Use with text pages 236–239.**

# Equivalent Fractions and Simplest Form

### To find equivalent fractions

| Multiply the numerator and denominator by the same number.  $\dfrac{3}{8} = \dfrac{9}{24}$ | Divide the numerator and denominator by a common factor. 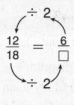 $\dfrac{12}{18} = \dfrac{6}{\square}$ $\dfrac{12}{18} = \dfrac{6}{9}$ | **Simplest form:** Divide numerator and denominator by greatest common factor (GCF).  $\dfrac{12}{18} = \dfrac{2}{3}$ |

**Complete.**

1. $\dfrac{5}{8} = \dfrac{10}{\square}$ 

2. $\dfrac{12}{15} = \dfrac{\square}{5}$ 

3. $\dfrac{9}{18} = \dfrac{1}{\square}$ 

4. $\dfrac{2}{3} = \dfrac{\square}{9}$

_____  _____  _____

5. $\dfrac{7}{10} = \dfrac{\square}{100}$ 

6. $\dfrac{21}{27} = \dfrac{7}{\square}$ 

7. $\dfrac{6}{30} = \dfrac{3}{\square}$ 

8. $\dfrac{10}{25} = \dfrac{\square}{50}$

_____  _____  _____

**Simplify each fraction.**

9. $\dfrac{22}{4}$ 

10. $\dfrac{20}{16}$ 

11. $\dfrac{22}{32}$ 

12. $\dfrac{45}{36}$

_____  _____  _____  _____

13. $\dfrac{35}{15}$ 

14. $\dfrac{42}{48}$ 

15. $\dfrac{30}{9}$ 

16. $\dfrac{40}{16}$

_____  _____  _____  _____

## Problem Solving

17. Write $0.98 as a fraction of a dollar in simplest form.

_____

**Show Your Work**

**Use with text pages 240–241.**

# Problem-Solving Strategy:
# Use Logical Reasoning

| | Ask Yourself |
|---|---|
| **Understand** | What facts do I know? |
| **Plan** | How can I organize what I know so that I can use logical thinking? |
| **Solve** | Can I draw a Venn diagram? |
| | Did I label the parts of my diagram? |
| | Did I find the factors of the two numbers? |
| **Look Back** | Does my answer meet all the given conditions? |
| | How can I check my answer? |

**Use logical thinking to solve each problem.**

**Show Your Work**

1. Joe and Anna collect football cards. The GCF of the numbers of cards in their collections is 15. Altogether Joe and Anna have 75 cards. If Joe has more cards than Anna, how many cards do they each have?

   _____

2. The LCM of two numbers is 100. The GCF of the numbers is 1. The sum of the numbers is 29. What are the numbers?

   _____

3. Fraction $\frac{r}{s} = \frac{5}{8}$. $r + s = 39$. What are $r$ and $s$?

   _____

**Use with text pages 242–245.**

# Relate Fractions, Mixed Numbers, and Decimals

| Decimals and Fractions | |
| --- | --- |
| Write a decimal as a fraction. | Write a fraction as a decimal. |
| $0.7 = \frac{7}{10}$ | $\frac{3}{4} = \frac{75}{100} = 0.75$ |
| $0.55 = \frac{55}{100} = \frac{11}{20}$ | $\frac{9}{10} = 0.9$ |

**Write each decimal as a fraction or mixed number in simplest form.**

1. 0.42      2. 7.5      3. 0.38      4. 0.01

_____      _____      _____      _____

5. 6.18      6. 2.2      7. 0.6      8. 1.01

_____      _____      _____      _____

**Write each fraction or mixed number as a decimal.**

9. $\frac{9}{10}$      10. $5\frac{7}{50}$      11. $2\frac{4}{5}$      12. $6\frac{1}{4}$

_____      _____      _____      _____

13. $\frac{4}{25}$      14. $\frac{19}{50}$      15. $3\frac{11}{20}$      16. $\frac{13}{25}$

_____      _____      _____      _____

## Problem Solving

**Show Your Work**

17. Write a decimal and a fraction to show what part of a dollar one penny represents. Write your answer in simplest form.

_____

**Use with text pages 246–247.**

Name _____ Date _____

# Compare and Order Fractions and Decimals

| **Different Ways to Compare 2.4, $2\frac{1}{4}$, and 2.04** | |
|---|---|
| **Way 1:** Write the mixed number as a decimal.<br><br>$2\frac{1}{4} = 2.25$<br><br>Compare the decimals.<br><br>$2.04 < 2.25 < 2.4$ | **Way 2:** Write the decimals as mixed numbers.<br><br>$2.4 = 2\frac{4}{10}$   $2.04 = 2\frac{4}{100}$<br><br>Rename with a common denominator.<br><br>$2\frac{4}{10} = 2\frac{40}{100}$   $2\frac{1}{4} = 2\frac{25}{100}$<br><br>Compare the mixed numbers.<br><br>$2\frac{4}{100} < 2\frac{25}{100} < 2\frac{40}{100}$ |

**Compare. Write >, <, or = for each ◯.**

1. $0.6 \bigcirc \frac{1}{5}$

2. $9.08 \bigcirc 9\frac{1}{5}$

3. $\frac{4}{5} \bigcirc 0.9$

4. $1\frac{7}{10} \bigcirc 1.07$

_____   _____   _____   _____

5. $2.5 \bigcirc 2\frac{1}{2}$

6. $1\frac{13}{20} \bigcirc 1.8$

7. $3.6 \bigcirc 3\frac{6}{100}$

8. $\frac{9}{25} \bigcirc 0.4$

_____   _____   _____   _____

**Order each set of numbers from least to greatest.**

9. $\frac{1}{2}, \frac{6}{10}, 0.2, 0.4$

10. $\frac{3}{10}, 0.75, 1.2, 1\frac{1}{10}$

_____   _____

11. $3.6, 3.55, 1.8, \frac{2}{10}$

12. $2.09, 2\frac{4}{5}, 2.5, 2\frac{9}{10}$

_____   _____

## Problem Solving

**Show Your Work**

13. On Monday, $\frac{4}{10}$ of the students bought lunch in the cafeteria. On Tuesday, 0.3 of the students bought lunch and on Wednesday, $\frac{3}{5}$ bought lunch. How would you list the days from least to most lunches purchased from the cafeteria?

_____

Use with text pages 248–251.

# Estimate With Fractions

| Estimate $\frac{4}{5} + \frac{1}{8} + \frac{11}{20}$. | Estimate $65\frac{3}{4} - 23\frac{1}{2}$. |
|---|---|
| Round the fractions to 0, $\frac{1}{2}$, or 1. | Use front-end estimation. |
| $\frac{4}{5}$ is close to 1. | $65\frac{3}{4}$ |
| $\frac{1}{8}$ is close to 0. | $- 23\frac{1}{2}$ |
| $\frac{11}{20}$ is close to $\frac{1}{2}$. | $\overline{\phantom{xx}40\phantom{xx}}$ |
| $1 + 0 + \frac{1}{2} = 1\frac{1}{2}$ | |

**Estimate the sum or difference. Name the method you used.**

1. $\frac{13}{15} - \frac{3}{5}$

2. $6\frac{1}{2} + 8\frac{2}{3}$

3. $\frac{9}{10} + \frac{7}{8}$

4. $45\frac{2}{3} - 34\frac{2}{7}$

5. $85\frac{5}{9} + 21\frac{1}{4}$

6. $\frac{6}{7} + \frac{2}{3} + \frac{1}{8}$

7. $13\frac{4}{5} + 74\frac{2}{3}$

8. $\frac{4}{9} + \frac{8}{15} + \frac{9}{10}$

9. $59\frac{3}{4} - 18\frac{5}{6}$

10. $\frac{6}{7} + \frac{2}{5} + \frac{5}{9} + \frac{1}{6}$

11. $84\frac{1}{5} + 37\frac{2}{3}$

12. $\frac{9}{20} + \frac{13}{15} + \frac{2}{11} + \frac{7}{8}$

## Problem Solving

**Show Your Work**

13. Meg made a quilt that is $50\frac{3}{4}$ inches long. She put $1\frac{7}{8}$ inches of trim along the edges of her quilt. About how long is it now?

_____

Use with text pages 256–257.

# Add Fractions With Like Denominators

Add $3\frac{6}{7} + 1\frac{5}{7}$.

| **Step 1:** Add the fractions. | **Step 2:** Add the whole numbers. | **Step 3:** Simplify. |
|---|---|---|
| $3\frac{6}{7}$ $+ 1\frac{5}{7}$ $\overline{\phantom{1}\frac{11}{7}}$ | $3\frac{6}{7}$ $+ 1\frac{5}{7}$ $\overline{4\frac{11}{7}}$ | $3\frac{6}{7}$ $+ 1\frac{5}{7}$ $\overline{4\frac{11}{7} = 5\frac{4}{7}}$ |

**Add. Write each sum in the simplest form.**

**1.** $4\frac{3}{9} + 1\frac{5}{9}$

_____

**2.** $5\frac{2}{8} + 2\frac{7}{8}$

_____

**3.** $\frac{5}{12} + \frac{11}{12}$

_____

**4.** $\frac{2}{3} + 1\frac{1}{3}$

_____

**5.** $\frac{8}{11} + \frac{7}{11}$

_____

**6.** $6\frac{1}{5} + 3\frac{4}{5}$

_____

**7.** $3\frac{7}{10}$ $+ 4\frac{9}{10}$

**8.** $\frac{7}{9}$ $+ \frac{7}{9}$

**9.** $5\frac{2}{3}$ $+ 4\frac{2}{3}$

**10.** $6\frac{5}{10}$ $+ 3\frac{3}{10}$

**11.** $7\frac{3}{4}$ $+ 6\frac{1}{4}$

**12.** $11\frac{9}{15}$ $+ 7\frac{3}{15}$

## Problem Solving

**13.** Tani jogged $1\frac{3}{4}$ km on Tuesday and $2\frac{3}{4}$ km on Thursday. How far did he jog altogether?

_____

**Show Your Work**

**Use with text pages 258–259.**

# Add Fractions With Unlike Denominators

Add $\frac{4}{5} + \frac{2}{3}$.

| **Step 1:** Use the LCD to find equivalent fractions. | **Step 2:** Add the fractions. | **Step 3:** Simplify. |
|---|---|---|
| $\frac{4}{5} = \frac{12}{15}$ $+ \frac{2}{3} = \frac{10}{15}$ | $\begin{array}{r} \frac{12}{15} \\ + \frac{10}{15} \\ \hline \frac{22}{15} \end{array}$ | $\frac{22}{15} = 1\frac{7}{15}$ |

**Add. Write each sum in simplest form.**

**1.** $\frac{2}{3} + \frac{2}{8}$

_____

**2.** $\frac{3}{4} + \frac{5}{8}$

_____

**3.** $\frac{9}{10} + \frac{3}{5}$

_____

**4.** $\frac{6}{7} + \frac{1}{2}$

_____

**5.** $\frac{5}{6} + \frac{7}{9}$

_____

**6.** $\frac{1}{3} + \frac{4}{10}$

_____

**7.** $\begin{array}{r} \frac{3}{10} \\ + \frac{9}{20} \\ \hline \end{array}$

**8.** $\begin{array}{r} \frac{6}{10} \\ + \frac{1}{4} \\ \hline \end{array}$

**9.** $\begin{array}{r} \frac{5}{8} \\ + \frac{5}{6} \\ \hline \end{array}$

**10.** $\begin{array}{r} \frac{2}{8} \\ + \frac{3}{4} \\ \hline \end{array}$

**11.** $\begin{array}{r} \frac{3}{7} \\ + \frac{1}{3} \\ \hline \end{array}$

**12.** $\begin{array}{r} \frac{9}{10} \\ + \frac{3}{15} \\ \hline \end{array}$

## Problem Solving

**13.** A chef used $\frac{3}{4}$ cup of water, $\frac{1}{2}$ cup of milk, and $\frac{1}{8}$ cup of orange juice in a recipe. How many cups of ingredients did she use altogether?

_____

**Show Your Work**

**Use with text pages 260–261.**

# Add Mixed Numbers With Unlike Denominators

Add $2\frac{1}{6} + 3\frac{2}{3} + 1\frac{1}{4}$.

**Step 1:** Use the LCD to find equivalent fractions.

$2\frac{1}{6} = 2\frac{2}{12}$

$3\frac{2}{3} = 3\frac{8}{12}$

$+ 1\frac{1}{4} = 1\frac{3}{12}$

**Step 2:** Add the fractions.

$2\frac{2}{12}$

$3\frac{8}{12}$

$+1\frac{3}{12}$

$\frac{13}{12}$

**Step 3:** Add the whole numbers. Simplify.

$2\frac{2}{12}$

$3\frac{8}{12}$

$+ 1\frac{3}{13}$

$6\frac{13}{12} = 7\frac{1}{12}$

**Add. Write each sum in simplest form.**

1. $3\frac{2}{3} + 1\frac{1}{4}$

2. $4\frac{1}{2} + 2\frac{3}{8}$

3. $7\frac{1}{3} + 3\frac{1}{2}$

4. $1\frac{6}{7} + 2\frac{1}{2}$

5. $6\frac{3}{5} + 4\frac{7}{10}$

6. $5\frac{2}{3} + 1\frac{3}{4}$

7. $9\frac{1}{2}$
   $+ 4\frac{2}{3}$

8. $5\frac{3}{8}$
   $+ 1\frac{3}{4}$

9. $1\frac{9}{10}$
   $+ 7\frac{4}{5}$

10. $4\frac{3}{6}$
    $2\frac{1}{3}$
    $+ 1\frac{3}{4}$

11. $2\frac{3}{9}$
    $4\frac{1}{2}$
    $+ 5\frac{2}{3}$

12. $8\frac{5}{8}$
    $7\frac{4}{5}$
    $+ 1\frac{3}{10}$

## Problem Solving

**Show Your Work**

13. Paulina used $4\frac{1}{2}$ yards of red cloth, $1\frac{3}{8}$ yards of white cloth, and $2\frac{3}{4}$ yards of blue cloth to make a costume. How much cloth did she use altogether?

_____

**Use with text pages 262–265.**

# Subtract With Like Denominators

Find $7 - 3\frac{4}{5}$.

**Step 1:** Rename the whole number.

$$7 = 6\frac{5}{5}$$
$$-3\frac{4}{5} = -3\frac{4}{5}$$

**Step 2:** Subtract the fractions.

$$6\frac{5}{5}$$
$$-3\frac{4}{5}$$
$$\overline{\phantom{-3}\frac{1}{5}}$$

**Step 3:** Subtract the whole numbers. Simplify.

$$6\frac{5}{5}$$
$$-3\frac{4}{5}$$
$$\overline{3\frac{1}{5}}$$

**Subtract. Write each difference in simplest form.**

1. $8\frac{1}{16} - 3\frac{7}{16}$

2. $9 - 3\frac{1}{4}$

3. $7\frac{3}{5} - 2\frac{4}{5}$

4. $6 - 1\frac{2}{3}$

5. $8\frac{3}{7} - 6\frac{3}{7}$

6. $5 - 4\frac{1}{9}$

7. $\frac{9}{10}$
$-\frac{4}{10}$

8. $\frac{7}{8}$
$-\frac{3}{8}$

9. $8\frac{4}{5}$
$-2\frac{1}{5}$

10. $10$
$-4\frac{2}{3}$

11. $3\frac{1}{2}$
$-1\frac{1}{2}$

12. $7\frac{5}{9}$
$-5\frac{2}{9}$

## Problem Solving

**Show Your Work**

13. Russell has 5 m of wire. He used $3\frac{3}{4}$ m for a project. How much wire is left?

_____

**Use with text pages 266–267.**

# Subtract Fractions With Unlike Denominators

Find $\frac{4}{5} - \frac{3}{10}$.

**Step 1:** Use the LCD to find equivalent fractions.

$$\frac{4}{5} = \frac{8}{10}$$
$$-\frac{3}{10} = -\frac{3}{10}$$

**Step 2:** Subtract.

$$\frac{8}{10}$$
$$-\frac{3}{10}$$
$$\overline{\frac{5}{10}}$$

**Step 3:** Simplify.

$$\frac{8}{10}$$
$$-\frac{3}{10}$$
$$\overline{\frac{5}{10}} = \frac{1}{2}$$

**Subtract. Write the difference in simplest form.**

1. $\frac{3}{4} - \frac{1}{3}$

2. $\frac{5}{8} - \frac{1}{4}$

3. $\frac{2}{3} - \frac{1}{5}$

_____

4. $\frac{5}{12} - \frac{1}{6}$

5. $\frac{8}{15} - \frac{1}{5}$

6. $\frac{9}{10} - \frac{1}{4}$

_____

7. $\frac{17}{20}$
   $-\frac{3}{5}$

8. $\frac{5}{6}$
   $-\frac{2}{3}$

9. $\frac{7}{9}$
   $-\frac{1}{3}$

10. $\frac{12}{15}$
    $-\frac{1}{5}$

11. $\frac{3}{4}$
    $-\frac{1}{6}$

12. $\frac{7}{10}$
    $-\frac{1}{4}$

## Problem Solving

13. Bella bought $\frac{3}{4}$ pound of nuts. Her family ate $\frac{1}{8}$ pound of the nuts. How much is left?

_____

**Show Your Work**

**Use with text pages 268–269.**

# Problem-Solving Strategy:
# Draw a Diagram

| | Ask Yourself |
|---|---|
| **Understand** | What facts do I know? |
| **Plan** | Did I draw a diagram? |
| **Solve** | How can I use my diagram to solve the problem? |
| **Look Back** | Did I solve the problem? |
| | Is my answer reasonable? |

**Draw a diagram to solve each problem.**

**Show Your Work**

1. The Hawks soccer team practiced three times this week. On Tuesday, the team practiced for $\frac{3}{4}$ hour. On Thursday, the team practiced for $\frac{1}{2}$ hour more than it did on Tuesday. On Saturday, the team practiced twice as long as it did on both Tuesday and Thursday combined. Altogether, how long did the Hawks practice this week?

   _____

2. The Hawks have 18 players. Boys make up $\frac{5}{6}$ of the team. How many girls are on the Hawks?

   _____

3. The first week of practice, the team practiced 4 times. On Monday, they practiced for $\frac{1}{2}$ hour. On Wednesday, they practiced $1\frac{1}{2}$ times as long as they did on Monday. On Thursday and Friday combined, they practiced 3 times as long as they did on Monday. Altogether, how long did the Hawks practice the first week?

   _____

**Use with text pages 270–272.**

# Subtract Mixed Numbers With Unlike Denominators

**Find $5\frac{1}{2} - 1\frac{7}{8}$.**

| **Step 1:** Use the LCD to find equivalent fractions. | **Step 2:** Rename the mixed numbers. | **Step 3:** Subtract and simplify. |
|---|---|---|
| $5\frac{1}{2} = 5\frac{4}{8}$ <br> $-1\frac{7}{8} = -1\frac{7}{8}$ | $5\frac{4}{8} = 4\frac{12}{8}$ <br> $-1\frac{7}{8} = -1\frac{7}{8}$ | $4\frac{12}{8}$ <br> $-1\frac{7}{8}$ <br><br> $3\frac{5}{8}$ |

**Subtract. Write each difference in simplest form.**

1.  $9\frac{1}{2}$
    $-3\frac{5}{7}$

2.  $7\frac{1}{8}$
    $-2\frac{3}{6}$

3.  $7\frac{1}{5}$
    $-2\frac{1}{8}$

4.  $4\frac{1}{4}$
    $-2\frac{5}{6}$

5.  $9\frac{1}{8}$
    $-2\frac{1}{3}$

6.  $5\frac{4}{5}$
    $-2\frac{1}{4}$

7.  $7\frac{15}{16} - 2\frac{4}{8}$

8.  $6\frac{1}{3} - 4\frac{5}{6}$

9.  $3\frac{1}{5} - 1\frac{9}{10}$

**Write >, <, or = for each ◯.**

10. $7 - 3\frac{4}{9} \bigcirc 8\frac{1}{2} - 3\frac{1}{6}$

11. $9\frac{2}{5} - 1\frac{4}{6} \bigcirc 10 - 2\frac{4}{15}$

12. $6\frac{3}{8} - 5\frac{3}{4} \bigcirc 5\frac{1}{4} - 3\frac{5}{8}$

13. $8\frac{3}{4} - 3\frac{4}{5} \bigcirc 5\frac{1}{3} - 1\frac{5}{6}$

## Problem Solving

**Show Your Work**

15. Zack has $3\frac{1}{4}$ ft of wood. Lance has $1\frac{3}{4}$ ft of wood. Zack cut a $\frac{7}{8}$ ft piece from his wood and gave it to Lance. Who has more wood now? Explain.

**Use with text pages 274–277.**

# Explore Addition and Subtraction With Decimals

Find 0.37 + 0.09.

| **Step 1:** Change the decimals to fractions. | **Step 2:** Add the fractions. | **Step 3:** Write the sum as a decimal. |
|---|---|---|
| $0.37 = \frac{37}{100}$ <br> $0.09 = \frac{9}{100}$ | $\frac{37}{100} + \frac{9}{100} = \frac{46}{100}$ | $\frac{46}{100} = 0.46$ |

**Change each decimal to a fraction. Model each addition and subtraction. Write each sum as a decimal.**

1. 0.18 + 0.5

2. 0.29 + 0.68

3. 0.4 + 0.87

_____    _____    _____

4. 0.56 + 0.98

5. 0.41 + 2.03

6. 5.17 + 3.65

_____    _____    _____

**Change each decimal to a fraction. Subtract. Write each difference as a decimal.**

7. 0.19 − 0.08

8. 0.7 − 0.5

9. 0.8 − 0.25

_____    _____    _____

10. 3.28 − 1.46

11. 2.5 − 1.72

12. 5.8 − 4.9

_____    _____    _____

## Problem Solving

Show Your Work

13. Paul jogged 3.25 miles, Rick jogged $3\frac{1}{3}$ miles, and Sean jogged $3\frac{1}{8}$ miles. List the boys from least to greatest distance jogged. Tell how you found your answer.

_____

**Use with text pages 282–283.**

# Add Decimals

**Find 3.8 + 0.95.**

| **Step 1:** Use the decimal points to line up the addends. Add zeros as needed.<br><br>3.80<br>+0.95 | **Step 2:** Add the hundredths.<br><br><br>3.80<br>+0.95<br>5 | **Step 3:** Add the tenths.<br><br>1<br>3.80<br>+0.95<br>.75 | **Step 4:** Add the ones.<br><br>1<br>3.80<br>+0.95<br>4.75 |

**Add. Use a calculator to check.**

1. $12.42
   + 9.79

2. 9.1
   +5.88

3. 7.11
   +6.93

4. 6.13
   +45.2

5. 1.08
   +36.94

6. .6.2
   +74.75

7. 12.3 + 4.07

8. 26.4 + 0.005

9. 1.004 + 32.7

_____

_____

_____

10. 8.1 + 54.06 + 0.002

11. 5.72 + 0.108 + 93.25

12. 8.004 + 0.9 + 12.3

_____

_____

_____

## Problem Solving

**Show Your Work**

13. Maxine has 4.5 m of wire. She uses 1.75 m for each floral wreath she makes. Does Maxine have enough wire to make three wreaths? Explain your answer.

_____

**Use with text pages 284–285.**

# Subtract Decimals

Find 46.2 − 8.75.

| **Step 1:** Use the decimal points to line up the digits. Add zeros as needed. | **Step 2:** Subtract the hundredths. | **Step 3:** Subtract the tenths. | **Step 4:** Subtract the ones and tens. |
|---|---|---|---|
| 46.20<br>− 8.75 | 110<br>46.2̸0<br>− 8.75<br>5 | 5 11<br>46.2̸0<br>− 8.75<br>.45 | 3 15<br>4̸6.2̸0<br>− 8.75<br>37.45 |

**Subtract. Add or use a calculator to check your answer.**

1. 7.3
   −1.5

2. 8.4
   −6.6

3. $23.55
   − 8.70

4. 11.4
   − 6.32

5. 3.08
   −0.946

6. 24.8
   − 7.005

7. 9.1 − 2.48

8. 6.04 − 3.9

9. $10 − 4.89

_____

_____

_____

10. 6.7 − 3.112

11. 11.4 − 3.3

12. $15.22 − 12.67

_____

_____

_____

## Problem Solving

**Show Your Work**

13. Tony bought two notebooks at $1.89 each. He paid for the notebooks with a $20 bill. How much change did he get?

_____

**Use with text pages 286–289.**

# Estimate Decimal Sums and Differences

| Ways to Estimate 8.21 − 3.5 | | |
|---|---|---|
| **Round to ones** | **Front-end Estimation** | **Round to tenths** |
| 8.217    8<br>−3.5   −4<br>─────<br>        4 | 8.217    8<br>−3.5   −3<br>─────<br>        5 | 8.217   8.2<br>−3.5  −3.5<br>─────<br>      4.7 |

**Estimate each sum or difference to the nearest tenth.**

**1.** 0.548 + 0.356      **2.** 0.721 + 0.894      **3.** 0.155 + 0.426      **4.** 0.659 + 0.121

_____      _____      _____      _____

**5.** 0.793 − 0.518      **6.** 0.409 − 0.316      **7.** 0.564 − 0.293      **8.** 0.917 − 0.462

_____      _____      _____      _____

**Estimate each sum or difference to the nearest whole number.**

**9.** 5.16 + 7.8      **10.** 21.8 + 6.33      **11.** 3.05 + 41.749      **12.** 16.08 + 7.4

_____      _____      _____      _____

**13.** 62.9 − 45.13      **14.** 17.6 − 13.2      **15.** 31.5 − 19.1      **16.** 4.26 − 0.978

_____      _____      _____      _____

## Problem Solving

**17.** Nancy said that 23.5 − 7.2 is about 31. Do you agree with her? Tell why or why not.

**Show Your Work**

_____

**Use with text pages 290–291.**

# Problem-Solving Decision:
# Choose a Method

**Solve. Explain which method you used.**

**Show Your Work**

1. Ross ran a mile in 6.28 minutes to win a race. Don finished second with a time of 6.55 minutes. How much faster was Ross than Don?

2. Clark ran in the same race. His time was 1.37 minutes more than Ross's time. How long did it take Clark to run the mile?

3. On their new track shoes, Randy's shoe laces are 12.5 in. long, and Sarah's shoe laces are 13.75 in. long. How much longer are Sarah's shoe laces?

**Use with text pages 292–293.**

# Model Multiplication

Find $\frac{1}{3} \times \frac{3}{4}$.

**Use a Model to Multiply Fractions**

**Step 1:** Draw a square.

**Step 2:** Use horizontal lines to separate it into thirds.

**Step 3:** Use vertical lines to separate it into fourths.

**Step 4:** Shade and label $\frac{1}{3}$ of the square.

**Step 5:** Shade and label $\frac{3}{4}$ of the square.

**Step 6:** Count the parts that are shaded twice. $\frac{1}{3} \times \frac{3}{4} = \frac{3}{12}$ or $\frac{1}{4}$

**Write the equation represented by each model. Write the answer in simplest form.**

1.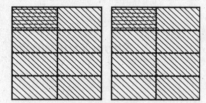

2.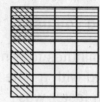

_____

_____

3.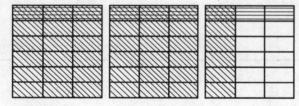

4.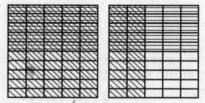

_____

_____

**Use models to find each product. Write the answer in simplest form.**

5. $4 \times \frac{1}{8}$

6. $1\frac{3}{4} \times \frac{2}{3}$

7. $2\frac{1}{2} \times \frac{1}{3}$

8. $6 \times \frac{3}{4}$

_____

_____

_____

_____

## Problem Solving

9. Jane had $1\frac{1}{2}$ yards of cloth. She cut it into 4 equal pieces. What is the size of one piece?

**Show Your Work**

_____

**Use with text pages 310–313.**

# Multiply Fractions

| Different Ways to Find $\frac{2}{3}$ of $\frac{6}{8}$ | |
|---|---|
| **Way 1:** Multiply, then simplify. | **Way 2:** Simplify, then multiply. |
| $\frac{2}{3} \times \frac{6}{8} = \frac{2 \times 6}{3 \times 8} = \frac{12}{24}$ | $\frac{2}{3} \times \frac{6}{8} = \frac{2 \times \overset{2}{\cancel{6}}}{\cancel{3} \times \cancel{2} \times 4} = \frac{2}{4}$ |
| $\frac{12}{24} \div \frac{12}{12} = \frac{1}{2}$ | $\frac{2 \div 2}{4 \div 2} = \frac{1}{2}$ |

**Multiply. Write your answer in simplest form.**

1. $\frac{1}{6} \times \frac{2}{3}$

2. $\frac{1}{8} \times 3$

3. $\frac{4}{9} \times \frac{3}{7}$

4. $\frac{2}{5} \times \frac{3}{5}$

5. $\frac{3}{4} \times \frac{5}{6}$

6. $\frac{1}{10} \times 5$

7. $\frac{4}{7} \times \frac{1}{4}$

8. $6 \times \frac{2}{3}$

9. $12 \times \frac{2}{3}$

10. $\frac{2}{5} \times \frac{1}{2}$

11. $\frac{8}{9} \times \frac{4}{5}$

12. $\frac{5}{6} \times 4$

## Problem Solving

**Show Your Work**

13. Laurence owns 20 balls. $\frac{4}{5}$ of the balls are larger than a baseball, and $\frac{1}{2}$ of those are soccer balls. How many soccer balls does Laurence own?

Use with text pages 314–315.

# Multiply With Mixed Numbers

Find $3\frac{1}{3} \times \frac{3}{5}$.

| **Step 1:** Write the mixed number as an improper fraction. | **Step 2:** Multiply. | **Step 3:** Simplify. |
| --- | --- | --- |
| $3\frac{1}{3} = \frac{10}{3}$ | $\frac{10}{3} \times \frac{3}{5} = \frac{30}{15}$ | $\frac{30}{15} \div \frac{15}{15} = \frac{2}{1} = 2$ |

**Multiply. Write each product in simplest form.**

1.  $1\frac{1}{5} \times \frac{3}{4}$

2.  $2\frac{1}{8} \times \frac{1}{4}$

3.  $3\frac{1}{6} \times \frac{2}{5}$

4.  $\frac{4}{5} \times 2\frac{1}{2}$

5.  $1\frac{3}{8} \times \frac{4}{5}$

6.  $2\frac{1}{5} \times \frac{3}{7}$

7.  $3\frac{1}{4} \times \frac{8}{9}$

8.  $\frac{4}{7} \times 2\frac{3}{4}$

9.  $1\frac{2}{5} \times \frac{1}{4}$

10.  $\frac{1}{6} \times 3\frac{1}{3}$

11.  $\frac{5}{9} \times 3\frac{2}{3}$

12.  $5\frac{1}{2} \times \frac{4}{7}$

## Problem Solving

**Show Your Work**

13. Kylie uses $1\frac{1}{2}$ cups of sugar for each batch of cookies she makes. How much sugar does she need to make 5 batches of cookies?

_____

Use with text pages 316–319.

Name _____    Date _____

# Model Division

Find $9 \div \frac{1}{3}$.

**Step 1:** Draw 9 wholes.

**Step 2:** Separate each whole into thirds.

**Step 3:** Count how many thirds are in 9 wholes. $9 \div \frac{1}{3} = 27$

**Write the equation represented by each model. Write the answer in simplest form.**

1.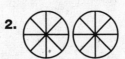

_____

2.

_____

3.

_____

4.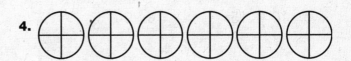

_____

**Divide. Check your answers.**

5. $\frac{3}{5} \div \frac{1}{5}$

_____

6. $\frac{5}{8} \div \frac{1}{8}$

_____

7. $\frac{7}{10} \div \frac{1}{10}$

_____

8. $\frac{5}{6} \div \frac{1}{6}$

_____

9. $\frac{10}{12} \div \frac{2}{12}$

_____

10. $\frac{4}{5} \div \frac{2}{5}$

_____

11. $\frac{9}{10} \div \frac{3}{10}$

_____

12. $\frac{6}{8} \div \frac{2}{8}$

_____

## Problem Solving

**Show Your Work**

13. Marie has 8 bracelets. She gave $\frac{1}{4}$ of her bracelets to her sister. How many bracelets does Marie have left?

_____

**Use with text pages 320–321.**

# Divide Fractions

Find $\frac{2}{3} \div \frac{6}{11}$.

**Step 1:** Rewrite as a multiplication problem using the reciprocal of the divisor.

$$\frac{2}{3} \div \frac{6}{11} = \frac{2}{3} \times \frac{11}{6}$$

**Step 2:** Find the product. Reduce if needed.

$$\frac{2}{3} \times \frac{11}{6} = \frac{22}{18} = 1\frac{2}{9}$$

**Divide. Write each answer in simplest form.**

1. $15 \div \frac{2}{3}$

2. $\frac{5}{8} \div \frac{5}{6}$

3. $\frac{3}{4} \div \frac{1}{3}$

4. $\frac{1}{2} \div \frac{7}{8}$

5. $10 \div 15$

6. $9 \div \frac{2}{3}$

7. $\frac{4}{5} \div \frac{1}{10}$

8. $\frac{11}{12} \div \frac{1}{4}$

9. $20 \div \frac{1}{2}$

10. $8 \div 12$

11. $\frac{3}{5} \div \frac{4}{7}$

12. $5 \div 7$

## Problem Solving

**Show Your Work**

13. One-fourth of the students in the fifth grade play baseball. If 30 students play baseball, how many students are in the fifth grade?

_____

**Use with text pages 322–323.**

# Divide Mixed Numbers

Find $3\frac{1}{3} \div 1\frac{1}{2}$.

---

**Step 1:** Write the mixed numbers as improper fractions.

$$3\frac{1}{3} \div 1\frac{1}{2} = \frac{10}{3} \div \frac{3}{2}$$

---

**Step 2:** Rewrite as a multiplication problem using the reciprocal of the divisor.

$$\frac{10}{3} \times \frac{2}{3} =$$

---

**Step 3:** Multiply. Simplify if needed.

$$\frac{10}{3} \times \frac{2}{3} = \frac{20}{9} = 2\frac{2}{9}$$

---

**Divide. Write each quotient in simplest form.**

1. $\frac{1}{3} \div 2\frac{1}{3}$

2. $\frac{5}{6} \div 1\frac{5}{6}$

3. $\frac{1}{2} \div 3\frac{1}{4}$

4. $1\frac{2}{5} \div 1\frac{3}{5}$

_____    _____    _____    _____

5. $\frac{1}{5} \div 3\frac{4}{5}$

6. $\frac{2}{3} \div 1\frac{1}{9}$

7. $\frac{3}{4} \div 1\frac{1}{2}$

8. $2\frac{1}{3} \div 1\frac{1}{6}$

_____    _____    _____    _____

9. $\frac{7}{8} \div 2\frac{3}{4}$

10. $\frac{5}{7} \div 2\frac{1}{2}$

11. $\frac{3}{5} \div 3\frac{1}{5}$

12. $\frac{4}{9} \div 5\frac{1}{3}$

_____    _____    _____    _____

## Problem Solving

**Show Your Work**

13. Taylor collected $4\frac{1}{3}$ gallons of rain water and used $2\frac{1}{2}$ gallons to water her indoor plants. What fraction of the water she collected did she use to water the plants?

_____

**Use with text pages 324–327.**

# Problem-Solving Decisions: Choose the Operation

| **Ask Yourself** | |
|---|---|
| **Understand** | What facts do I know? |
| **Plan** | What key words are in the problem? |
| **Solve** | Which operation will I use to solve the problem? |
| **Look Back** | Did I solve the problem? Is my answer reasonable? |

**Show Your Work**

1. Theo's bedroom measures $12\frac{3}{4}$ ft by $9\frac{2}{3}$ ft. What is the difference between the length and width of the room?

   _____

2. Theo wants some wallpaper for his room. One wallpaper originally cost $8 a roll. Now it is on sale for $\frac{3}{4}$ the regular price. If Theo buys 5 rolls, how will much he pay?

   _____

3. Another wallpaper regularly costs $6 a roll. But if Theo buys 9 rolls, he will get $\frac{1}{3}$ off the regular price of each roll. How much will 9 rolls cost Theo?

   _____

4. If Theo's parents pay $\frac{1}{4}$ of the cost of the second wallpaper, how much will Theo pay?

   _____

**Use with text pages 328–329.**

# Explore Multiplication

Find $\frac{1}{4}$ of 1.2.

| **Step 1:** Change 1.2 to a mixed number. | **Step 2:** Write the mixed number as an improper fraction. | **Step 3:** Multiply. Simplify, if needed. |
|---|---|---|
| $1.2 = 1\frac{2}{10}$ or $1\frac{1}{5}$ | $1\frac{1}{5} = \frac{6}{5}$ | $\frac{1}{4} \times \frac{6}{5} = \frac{6}{20} = \frac{3}{10}$ |

**Use models or fraction strips to multiply. Write each product as a decimal.**

1. $0.3 \times 0.6$

2. $0.9 \times 0.6$

3. $1.4 \times 0.8$

_____

4. $2.5 \times 0.4$

5. $1.3 \times 0.7$

6. $1.7 \times 0.2$

_____

7. $0.7 \times 0.7$

8. $0.5 \times 0.8$

9. $2.2 \times 0.3$

_____

10. $3.1 \times 0.4$

11. $2.6 \times 0.2$

12. $1.7 \times 0.9$

_____

## Problem Solving

**Show Your Work**

13. Lydia worked 6.5 hours on Saturday and 3.5 hours on Sunday. Rafael worked twice as long as Lydia did. How long did Lydia and Rafael work altogether?

_____

**Use with text pages 334–335.**

# Multiply Whole Numbers and Decimals

**Multiply.** $4 \times \$1.89 = s$

| **Step 1:** Estimate the product. | **Step 2:** Multiply. | **Step 3:** Insert decimal point. | **Step 4:** Compare with estimate. |
|---|---|---|---|
| $4 \times \$2 = \$8$ | $\begin{array}{r} 189 \\ \times\ \ 4 \\ \hline 756 \end{array}$ | $\begin{array}{r} \$1.89 \\ \times\ \ \ \ 4 \\ \hline \$7.56 \end{array}$<br><br>2 decimal places<br>0 decimal places<br>2 decimal places | $\$8$ is close to $\$7.56$. |

**Find each product.**

1. $5 \times 2.2$

2. $3 \times 0.12$

3. $2.75 \times 7$

_____

_____

_____

4. $12.5 \times 4$

5. $8 \times 4.2$

6. $14.1 \times 2$

_____

_____

_____

7. $7.6 \times 3$

8. $9 \times 3.9$

9. $5.2 \times 7$

_____

_____

_____

10. $3.172 \times 5$

11. $14 \times 0.28$

12. $17 \times 9.5$

_____

_____

_____

## Problem Solving

**13.** Last week, Felicia worked 4.5 hours on Monday and Wednesday. She worked 6.5 hours on Tuesday and Thursday. If she earns $7.50 an hour, how much did Felicia earn last week?

**Show Your Work**

_____

**Use with text pages 336–337.**

# Estimate Products

| Ways to Estimate 228 × 0.77 | | |
|---|---|---|
| **Round the numbers.** | **Round to lesser numbers.** | **Use fractions.** |
| 228 rounds to 200 | 228 rounds to 200 | 228 is about 200 |
| 0.77 rounds to 0.8 | 0.77 rounds to 0.7 | 0.77 is about $\frac{3}{4}$ |
| $200 \times 0.8 = 160$ | $200 \times 0.7 = 140$ | $\frac{3}{4}$ of 200 is 150 |

**Estimate each product.**

1. $13 \times 0.47$

2. $5.96 \times 3$

3. $4 \times 2.89$

_____

_____

_____

4. $3 \times 3.98$

5. $9.87 \times 12$

6. $3.075 \times 15$

_____

_____

_____

7. $4.46 \times 3$

8. $1.52 \times 23$

9. $5 \times 3.7$

_____

_____

_____

10. $0.124 \times 8$

11. $\$4.79 \times 14$

12. $\$2.17 \times 6$

_____

_____

_____

## Problem Solving

**Show Your Work**

13. Melissa is renting chairs for a party.
Each chair rents for $2.19. About
how much will it cost Melissa to rent
21 chairs?

_____

**Use with text pages 338–339.**

# Multiply Decimals

**Find 0.7 × 0.3.**

| **Step 1:** Multiply. Ignore the decimal points. | **Step 2:** Place the decimal point in the product. |
|---|---|
| $\begin{array}{r} 7 \\ \times 3 \\ \hline 21 \end{array}$ | $\begin{array}{r} 0.7 \\ \times 0.3 \\ \hline 0.21 \end{array}$   1 decimal place<br>1 decimal place<br>2 decimal places |

**Multiply.**

**1.** 0.7 × 0.2

**2.** 0.9 × 0.3

**3.** 0.32 × 0.5

_____

_____

_____

**4.** 0.3 × 6.2

**5.** 1.25 × 4.7

**6.** 0.6 × 5.4

_____

_____

_____

**7.** 2.65 × 0.29

**8.** 1.52 × 23

**9.** 1.57 × 6.6

_____

_____

_____

**Compare. Write >, <, or =.**

**10.** 0.4 × 6.1 ◯ 12.2 × 0.2

**11.** 3.5 × 1.7 ◯ 4.6 × 1.8

**12.** 0.9 × 5.6 ◯ 2.2 × 1.7

**13.** 0.4 × 3.8 ◯ 7.6 × 0.2

## Problem Solving

**14.** Jerome bought 1.4 pounds of string beans for $0.85 per pound. How much did he pay for string beans?

**Show Your Work**

_____

**Use with text pages 340–343.**

# Zeros in the Product

Find 0.02 × 0.04.

| **Step 1:** Multiply. Ignore the decimal points. | **Step 2:** Place the decimal point in the product. |
|---|---|
| 0.02<br>×0.04<br>8 | 0.02    2 decimal places<br>×0.04   2 decimal places<br>0.0008  4 decimal places |

**Multiply. Write zeros in front of the whole number to place the decimal point correctly.**

1.  0.07
    × 0.2

2.  0.03
    × 0.9

3.  0.005
    × 0.3

4.  0.002
    × 0.08

5.  0.006
    × 0.09

6.  0.025
    × 0.7

7.  0.04
    ×0.01

8.  0.03
    × 0.5

9. 0.051 × 0.06

10. 0.009 × 0.04

11. 0.08 × 0.005

12. 0.6 × 0.001

_____  _____    _____  _____

## Problem Solving

**Show Your Work**

13. In the Turtle Trot race, a turtle travels at the rate of 0.09 miles per hour. How far will the turtle travel in 0.40 hours?

_____

**Use with text pages 344–345.**

# Problem-Solving Decisions:
# Reasonable Answers

**Ask Yourself**

| | |
|---|---|
| **Understand** | What is the problem? |
| | What facts do I know? |
| **Plan** | Which operation will I use to solve the problem? |
| **Solve** | Are my calculations correct? |
| **Look Back** | Did I solve the problem? |
| | Is my answer reasonable? |

**Solve. Explain why the answer is reasonable or unreasonable.**

**Show Your Work**

1. Alvin earns $80. He plans to put 0.4 of that money in the bank and give his mother 0.2 of it. Alvin figures he will have $55 left over. Is he correct?

   _____

2. Alvin wants to buy a new video game system that costs $299. He plans to save $28.50 a week for the system. Alvin rounded the numbers to estimate how long it will take him to buy the system. He says he will have enough money after 10 weeks. Is he correct?

   _____

**Use with text pages 346–347.**

# Explore Division with Decimals

**Find 8 ÷ 0.25.**

**Step 1:** Write 8 and 0.25 as fractions. $8 \div \frac{1}{4}$

**Step 2:** Draw 8 circles to model 8 wholes.

**Step 3:** Separate each whole into four equal parts.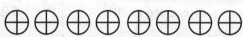

**Step 4:** Count the number of $\frac{1}{4}$s in all 8 wholes. $8 \div \frac{1}{4} = 32$

**Model the division, and write the quotient in decimal form.**

**1.** $6 \div 0.25$        **2.** $9 \div 0.5$        **3.** $4 \div 0.4$        **4.** $7 \div 0.2$

_____        _____        _____        _____

**5.** $12 \div 0.4$        **6.** $3 \div 0.2$        **7.** $8 \div 0.5$        **8.** $2 \div 0.1$

_____        _____        _____        _____

**9.** $5 \div 0.2$        **10.** $6 \div 0.25$        **11.** $4 \div 0.2$        **12.** $8 \div 0.2$

_____        _____        _____        _____

## Problem Solving

**Show Your Work**

**13.** A machine makes 24 donuts every 0.25 hour. At this rate, how many donuts are made in two hours?

_____

**Use with text pages 352–353.**

Name _____  Date _____

# Estimate Quotients

Estimate 71 ÷ 0.28.

| Step 1: Round the dividend to a number that is easy to work with.<br><br>71 is close to 70 | Step 2: Change the decimal to an equivalent fraction.<br><br>0.28 is close to 0.25<br>$0.25 = \frac{1}{4}$ | Step 3: Divide.<br><br>$70 \div \frac{1}{4} = 280$ |
|---|---|---|

**Estimate each quotient.**

1. 64 ÷ 0.48    2. 18.3 ÷ 0.31    3. 17 ÷ 0.19    4. 5.4 ÷ 0.21

_____    _____    _____    _____

5. 11.9 ÷ 0.82    6. 7.1 ÷ 0.214    7. 9.6 ÷ 0.53    8. 43.1 ÷ 0.792

_____    _____    _____    _____

9. 5.7 ÷ 0.32    10. 11.66 ÷ 0.2    11. 4.13 ÷ 0.802    12. 9 ÷ 0.247

_____    _____    _____    _____

## Problem Solving

**Show Your Work**

13. The Hawks soccer team has won 0.4 of the games they've played. If the team has won 2 games, how many games have the Hawks played?

_____

**Use with text pages 354–355.**

# Mental Math: Multiply and Divide by Powers of 10

| | |
|---|---|
| $0.0009 \times 10^1 = 0.009$ | $78 \div 10^1 = 7.8$ |
| $0.0009 \times 10^2 = 0.09$ | $78 \div 10^2 = 0.78$ |
| $0.0009 \times 10^3 = 0.9$ | $78 \div 10^3 = 0.078$ |
| $0.0009 \times 10^4 = 9$ | $78 \div 10^4 = 0.0078$ |

**Multiply or divide using patterns.**

**1.** $45.8 \times 10^2$  **2.** $8.3 \div 10^1$  **3.** $0.755 \times 10^3$  **4.** $0.66 \div 10^2$

_____   _____   _____   _____

**5.** $1.624 \times 10^3$  **6.** $9.21 \div 10^1$  **7.** $0.38 \times 10^2$  **8.** $57.9 \div 10^1$

_____   _____   _____   _____

**9.** $2,615 \times 10^1$  **10.** $1.52 \div 10^1$  **11.** $3.73 \times 10^2$  **12.** $9,800 \div 10^3$

_____   _____   _____   _____

## Problem Solving

**Show Your Work**

**13.** The distance between two stars is $3.45 \times 10^3$ miles. What is the distance expressed in standard form?

_____

**Use with text pages 356–357.**

# Divide a Decimal by a Whole Number

Find 4.2 ÷ 7.

$$
\begin{array}{r}
6 \\
7\overline{)42} \\
-42 \\
\hline
0
\end{array}
$$

**Step 1:** Divide the dividend, disregarding the decimal point.

$$
\begin{array}{r}
0.6 \\
7\overline{)4.2} \\
-4.2 \\
\hline
0
\end{array}
$$

**Step 2:** Place a decimal point in the quotient above the decimal point in the dividend.

**Divide and check.**

**1.** $9\overline{)8.1}$   **2.** $5\overline{)5.75}$   **3.** $7\overline{)18.2}$   **4.** $6\overline{)0.012}$

**5.** $2.4 \div 3$   **6.** $0.56 \div 8$   **7.** $21.06 \div 9$   **8.** $7.5 \div 5$

**9.** $4\overline{)25.92}$   **10.** $2\overline{)6.01}$   **11.** $7\overline{)3.22}$   **12.** $8\overline{)1.68}$

## Problem Solving

**Show Your Work**

**13.** A sailboat travels 24.9 miles in 3 hours. What is its average speed in miles per hour?

_____

**Use with text pages 358–361.**

# Write Zeros in the Dividend

Find 8.5 ÷ 2.

```
   4 2
2)8.5
  −8
   0 5
  −0 4
     1
```

**Step 1:** Divide as though the dividend were a whole number.

```
   4.25
2)8.50
  −8
   0 5
  −0 4
    10
   −10
     0
```

**Step 2:** Write a 0 in hundredths place. Continue dividing. Put a decimal point in the quotient above the decimal point in the dividend.

**Divide and check using a calculator or estimation.**

1. 2)6.9

2. 4)50

3. 5)4.7

4. 8)92

5. 8.6 ÷ 4

6. 18.6 ÷ 8

7. 5.44 ÷ 5

8. 14.1 ÷ 6

**Compare. Write >, <, or = for each ◯.**

9. 0.75 ÷ 6 ◯ 1.08 ÷ 8

10. 9.8 ÷ 4 ◯ 14.7 ÷ 6

11. 1.46 ÷ 4 ◯ 2.19 ÷ 6

12. 18 ÷ 8 ◯ 12.9 ÷ 6

## Problem Solving

**Show Your Work**

13. Vera cut a board 87.4 cm long into 4 equal pieces. How long is each piece?

**Use with text pages 362–365.**

# Repeating Decimals

Change $\frac{7}{22}$ to a decimal.

**Step 1:** Divide until the quotient ends or repeats.

**Step 2:** Put a decimal point in the quotient directly over the decimal point in the dividend.

**Step 3:** Write a bar over the parts of the quotient that repeats.

$$\frac{7}{22} = 0.3\overline{18}$$

```
        .31818
22)7.00000
  - 66
    40
  - 22
    180
  - 176
     40
   - 22
    180
  - 176
      4
```

**Change each fraction to decimal form.**

1. $\frac{8}{11}$ _____

2. $\frac{7}{12}$ _____

3. $\frac{4}{9}$ _____

4. $\frac{10}{22}$ _____

5. $\frac{20}{24}$ _____

6. $\frac{21}{36}$ _____

7. $\frac{2}{45}$ _____

8. $\frac{7}{30}$ _____

9. $\frac{2}{18}$ _____

10. $\frac{5}{27}$ _____

11. $\frac{11}{33}$ _____

12. $\frac{13}{45}$ _____

## Problem Solving

**Show Your Work**

13. Ryan has had 7 hits in his last 12 at bat. How much more or less than a 0.500 batting average does he have?

_____

**Use with text pages 366–367.**

# Divide a Decimal by a Decimal

**Find 3.75 ÷ 1.5.**

| **Step 1:** Multiply the divisor and dividend by the same power of 10 so that the divisor is a whole number. | **Step 2:** Divide. Place a decimal point in the quotient over the decimal point in the dividend. | $\begin{array}{r} 2.5 \\ 15\overline{)37.5} \\ -30 \phantom{.5} \\ \hline 7\,5 \\ -7\,5 \\ \hline 0 \end{array}$ |
|---|---|---|
| $1.5\overline{)3.75} \longrightarrow 15\overline{)37.5}$ | | |

**Divide. Round to the nearest hundredth. Check that your answer is reasonable.**

1. $2.4\overline{)9.984}$      2. $0.4\overline{)20.8}$      3. $0.4\overline{)0.28}$      4. $0.5\overline{)4.25}$

5. $0.2\overline{)5.6}$      6. $0.06\overline{)0.018}$      7. $7.2\overline{)25.2}$      8. $1.6\overline{)3.44}$

9. $3.6\overline{)20.88}$      10. $0.9\overline{)14.76}$      11. $0.8\overline{)5.76}$      12. $1.4\overline{)8.82}$

## Problem Solving

**Show Your Work**

13. An overseas phone call costs $7.44 for 24.8 minutes. What was the price per minute of the call?

_____

**Use with text pages 368–369.**

# Problem-Solving Application:
# Decide How to Write the Quotient

| | **Ask Yourself** |
|---|---|
| **Understand** | What is the problem? |
| | What facts do I know? |
| **Plan** | Which operation will I use to solve the problem? |
| **Solve** | What does the remainder represent? |
| **Look Back** | Does my answer make sense? |

**Solve. Explain how you used each remainder.**

**Show Your Work**

1. A scout troop is making a holiday display. The display contains 175 roses. The scouts will buy the flowers from a florist who sells roses in boxes of twelve. What is the fewest number of boxes the scouts should buy?

_____

2. The scouts want to give their troop leader a gift that costs $48. If the 15 troop members split the cost evenly, how much will each person contribute?

_____

**Use with text pages 370–373.**

# Points, Lines, and Rays

**Name each figure.**

1. R •———————→ S

_____

2. M •———————• N

_____

3. • J

_____

4. ←—•———————•—→ P ————— Q

_____

**Describe each pair of lines. Use symbols if possible.**

5.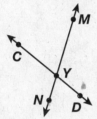

_____

6. G •———• H
   K •———• L

_____

**Draw and label each figure.**

7. Ray BC

_____

8. Point Q

_____

9. Line RT

_____

10. Ray AB

_____

11. Plane XYZ

_____

12. Line segment CD

_____

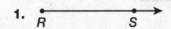 **Problem Solving**

**Show Your Work**

13. Line AB is perpendicular to line MN.
    How many right angles are formed
    where the two lines meet?

_____

**Use with text pages 390–391.**

# Measure, Draw, and Classify Angles

| Classifying Angles | |
| --- | --- |
| **Right angle:** | equal to 90° |
| **Acute angle:** | greater than 0° and less than 90° |
| **Obtuse angle:** | greater than 90° and less than 180° |
| **Straight angle:** | equal to 180° |

**In Exercises 1–4, use symbols to name each angle three different ways.**

1.

_____

2.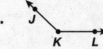

_____

3.

_____

4.

_____

**Classify each angle as acute, obtuse, straight, or right.**

5.

_____

6.

_____

7.

_____

**Use a protractor to draw an angle having each measure.
Classify each angle as right, acute, obtuse, or straight.**

8. 125°          9. 180°          10. 65°          11. 90°

_____     _____     _____     _____

## Problem Solving

**Show Your Work**

12. How many right angles equal one
    straight angle?

_____

**Use with text pages 392–395.**

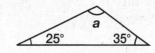

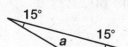
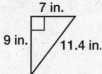

# Triangles

| **Classifying Triangles** | |
|---|---|
| **By lengths of their sides:** | **By their angle measures:** |
| Equilateral — all sides are the same length. | Right — one right angle |
| Isosceles — two sides are the same length. | Acute — all acute angles |
| Scalene — No sides are the same length. | Obtuse — one obtuse angle |

**Classify each triangle in two ways.**

1.  6 cm  6 cm
    6 cm

    _____

2.  35 miles
    16 miles   16 miles

    _____

3.  7 in.
    9 in.   11.4 in.

    _____

4.  6 m
    8 m
    7 m

    _____

**Write an expression to represent _a_. Then find the value of _a_.**

5.  _a_
    55°

    _____

6.  60°
    60°  _a_

    _____

7.  15°
    15°
    _a_

    _____

8.  _a_
    25°   35°

    _____

## Problem Solving

9. Can a triangle contain a right angle and
   an obtuse angle? Tell why or why not.

   _____

**Show Your Work**

**Use with text pages 396–397.**

Name _____ Date _____

# Congruence

| Different Ways to Check for Congruence | |
|---|---|
| **By tracing:** | **By measuring:** |
| Trace one figure. | Use a ruler to measure the sides of the figures. |
| Place the tracing on top of the other figure. | Use a protractor to measure the figures' angles. |
| If they are the same size and shape, the figures are congruent. | If the measurements are the same, the figures are congruent. |

**Use a ruler to measure the sides and a protractor to measure the angles of each figure. Mark the congruent sides and angles.**

1.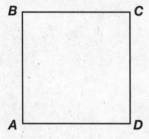

   _____

2. 

   G

   H          J

   _____

**Use the diagram to answer the questions. Explain your reasoning.**

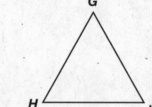

3. What is the length of side $\overline{RS}$?

   _____

4. What is the measure of $\angle T$?

   _____

5. What is the measure of $\angle S$?

   _____

6. What is the measure of $\angle R$?

   _____

## Problem Solving

**Show Your Work**

7. If two squares have the same side
   lengths, are the squares necessarily
   congruent? Tell why or why not.

   _____

**Use with text pages 398–399.**

Name _____  Date _____

# Quadrilaterals and Other Polygons

**Ask Yourself**

• How many sides does the polygon have?      • Are any sides congruent?

• Are any sides parallel?                                    • Are any angles congruent?

**Classify each polygon in as many ways as you can.**

**1.**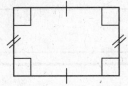

_____

**2.**

_____

**3.**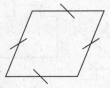

_____

**4.** 

_____

**Write *polygon* or *not a polygon* to classify each figure. Find the measure of each missing angle.**

**5.**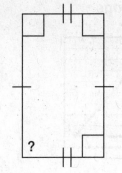

_____

**6.**

_____

## Problem Solving

**Show Your Work**

**7.** If every square is a rectangle, is every rectangle also a square? Explain.

_____

**Use with text pages 400–403.**

Name _____ Date _____

# Rotations, Reflections, and Translations

| | |
|---|---|
| **Transformation:** | changes the position of a plane figure |
| **Reflection:** | figure is flipped over a line |
| **Rotation:** | figure turns around a point |
| **Translation:** | figure is moved a given distance in a given direction |

**Tell whether each figure shows a translation, reflection, or rotation. If a figure shows a rotation, name the number of degrees of rotation.**

1.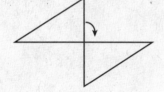

2.

3.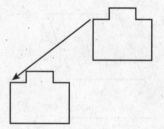

_____   _____   _____

**Copy each figure on grid paper. Then complete the given transformations.**

4.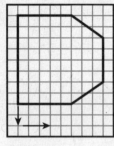

translation

5.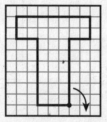

rotation of 90° clockwise

6.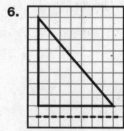

reflection

**Problem Solving**

7. What happens when you translate a figure down three units, then up three units?

_____

**Show Your Work**

**Use with text pages 404–407.**

Name _____  Date _____

# Problem-Solving Strategy:
# Make a Model

<table>
<tr><td colspan="2" align="center">**Ask Yourself**</td></tr>
<tr><td>**Understand**</td><td>What facts do I know?</td></tr>
<tr><td>**Plan**</td><td>Did I make a model?<br>Does my model represent the pattern exactly?</td></tr>
<tr><td>**Solve**</td><td>Did I use transformations to test if the patterns fit together?<br>Did I repeat the pattern enough so I could see if it tessellated?<br>Did I tile the plane without gaps or overlaps?</td></tr>
<tr><td>**Look Back**</td><td>Did I solve the problem?</td></tr>
</table>

**Make a model to solve each problem.**

**Show Your Work**

1. Bill said that a regular hexagon will tesselate. Is he right or wrong? How do you know?

_____

2. Leah said this figure will tesselate. Do you agree with her? Explain.

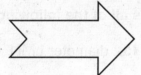

_____

3. Pedro said that this diamond will tesselate. Do you agree with him? Tell why.

_____

**Use with text pages 408–411.**

# Circles

| Radius: | a segment that connects the center of a circle to any point on the circle |
| --- | --- |
| Diameter: | a segment that connects two points on the circle and passes through its center |
| Chord: | any segment that connects two points on the circle |
| Central angle: | an angle with its vertex at the center of the circle |

**Use symbols to identify the following parts of this circle.**

1. chords

2. radii

_____

_____

3. central angles

4. diameter

_____

_____

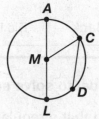

**Classify each figure as radius, diameter, chord, or central angle. Indicate if more than one term applies.**

5. $\overline{YX}$

6. $\overline{QR}$

7. $\angle YZQ$

_____

_____

_____

8. $\overline{RZ}$

9. $\overline{QZ}$

10. $\angle RZX$

_____

_____

_____

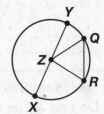

**On a separate sheet of paper, construct a circle that contains all of the following.**

11. center M

12. radius MN

13. diameter LMN

14. chord KL

15. central angle KML

16. chord JK

## Problem Solving

17. If a central angle measures 180°, what is it called?

**Show Your Work**

_____

**Use with text pages 412–413.**

# Symmetry

**Trace each figure, and turn it. Write *yes* or *no* to tell if it has rotational symmetry. If it does, tell how many degrees you turned it.**

1.

_____

2.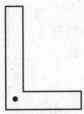

_____

3.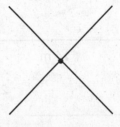

_____

**Trace each figure and fold it. Write *yes* or *no* to tell if it has line symmetry. If it does, write the number of lines of symmetry it has. Then sketch the figure, and its line(s) of symmetry.**

4.

_____

5.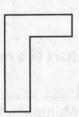

_____

6.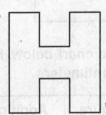

_____

**Use a compass, a protractor, and another sheet of paper to draw these figures.**

7. A figure with two lines of symmetry

8. A figure with rotational symmetry

9. A figure with no lines of symmetry

## Problem Solving

10. How many lines of symmetry does a square have?

_____

**Show Your Work**

**Use with text pages 414–417.**

Name _____  Date _____

# Perimeter

| Formulas for Perimeter | |
|---|---|
| **Perimeter of a square**   $P = 4s$ | **Perimeter of a rectangle**   $P = 2l + 2w$ |

**Find the perimeter or the missing length.**

1. _____
   8 m
   14 m

2. _____
   6.5 ft
   4.25 ft

3. _____
   $2\frac{3}{4}$ ft
   $2\frac{3}{4}$ ft

4. _____
   $P = 22$ ft
   7 ft

5. _____
   6.5 yd   $P = 26$ yd

6. _____
   $P = 17.6$ m
   3.6 m

**Complete the chart below. Each figure in the chart is a regular figure with sides of 4 centimeters.**

| Regular Figure | Addition Expression | Multiplication Expression | Perimeter |
|---|---|---|---|
| **7.** triangle | | | |
| **8.** pentagon | | | |
| **9.** heptagon | | | |

## Problem Solving

**Show Your Work**

10. Mae's bedroom is 12 feet long and 9 feet wide. She is putting a border along all four walls of the room. The border is sold in two yard packs. What is the least number of packs Mae can buy to have enough border for her room?

_____

Use with text pages 422–423.

# Problem-Solving Strategy:
# Find a Pattern

| | **Ask Yourself** |
|---|---|
| **Understand** | What facts do I know? |
| **Plan** | What kinds of patterns can I look for? |
| **Solve** | Did I figure out how each shape in the pattern was different from the shape before it? |
| | Did I describe the pattern? |
| | Did I continue the pattern? |
| **Look Back** | How can I check the answer? |

**Use a pattern to solve each problem.**

**Show Your Work**

1. Claudio made this pattern.

 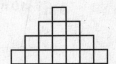

   If the pattern continues, how many small squares
   will be in the sixth shape?

   _____

2. There are 12 flowers in the first row of a garden.
   The second row has 20 flowers, the third row has
   30 flowers, and the fourth row has 42 flowers.
   How many flowers are likely in the sixth row?

   _____

3. Find the next three times that the star will be
   in the same position as it is in the first shape.

   _____

**Use with text pages 424–427.**

Name _____ Date _____

# Algebra: Area of a Parallelogram

| Formulas for Area | |
|---|---|
| Area of a rectangle    $A = l \times w$ | Area of a parallelogram    $A = b \times h$ |

**Find the area of each figure.**

1.

5 m    6 m
12 m

_____

2.

2 m
8 m    6 m

_____

3.

3 ft    4 ft
15 ft

_____

4.

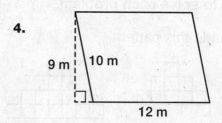

9 m    10 m
12 m

_____

5.

8 yd
13 yd

_____

6.

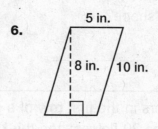

5 in.
8 in.    10 in.

_____

## Problem Solving

7. Identify the length and width of three different rectangles that have an area of 24cm².

_____

**Show Your Work**

**Use with text pages 428–431.**

# Algebra: Area of a Triangle

| Find the area of a triangle with a base of 8 cm and a height of 6 cm. |
| --- |
| $A = \frac{1}{2} \times b \times h$      $A = \frac{1}{2} \times 8 \times 6$      $A = 24$ cm$^2$ |

**Find the area of each triangle.**

**1.**

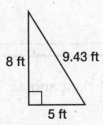

8 ft   9.43 ft

5 ft

_____

**2.**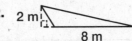

2 m

8 m

_____

**3.**

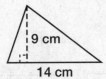

9 cm

14 cm

_____

**4.**

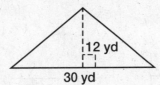

12 yd

30 yd

_____

**5.**

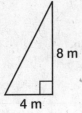

8 m

4 m

_____

**6.**

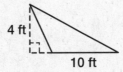

4 ft

10 ft

_____

## Problem Solving

**Show Your Work**

**7.** A triangle has a base of 3.6 cm and an area of 22.32 cm$^2$. What is the height of this triangle?

_____

**Use with text pages 432–433.**

# Perimeter and Area of Irregular Figures

| Finding the Perimeter of an Irregular Figure | Finding the Area of an Irregular Figure |
|---|---|
| **Step 1:** Find any missing lengths. | **Step 1:** Divide the figure into simple figures. |
| **Step 2:** Add the lengths of all the sides. | **Step 2:** Use formulas to find the area of each simple figure. |
| | **Step 3:** Add the areas. |

**Find the perimeter and area of each figure. All intersecting sides meet at right angles.**

1. 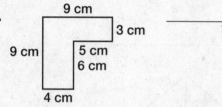  _____

2. 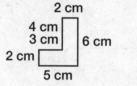  _____

3. 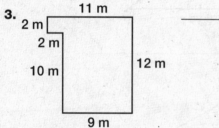  _____

4. 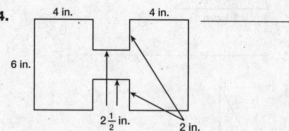  _____

5. 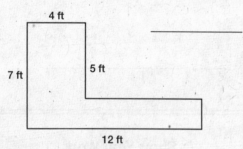  _____

6. 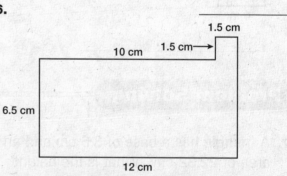  _____

## Problem Solving

**7.** Draw two irregular figures each with a perimeter of 20 inches.

**Show Your Work**

_____

**Use with text pages 434–437.**

# Algebra: Circumference of a Circle

| How to Find Circumference of a Circle | |
|---|---|
| **If you know the diameter:** $C = \pi d$ | **If you know the radius:** $C = 2\pi r$ |

Express each circumference as a fraction or mixed number in simplest form. Use $\frac{22}{7}$ for $\pi$.

1. 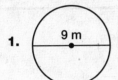 9 m  _____

2.  14 m _____

3.  10 in. _____

4.  $\frac{1}{4}$ m _____

5.  $2\frac{1}{2}$ ft _____

6.  $\frac{9}{7}$ yd _____

## Problem Solving

**Show Your Work**

7. The diameter of a watch face is 3 cm. What is the circumference of the watch face?

_____

**Use with text pages 438–441.**

# Solid Figures

| | |
|---|---|
| **face:** | a flat surface of a solid figure |
| **edge:** | line segment formed where two faces meet |
| **vertex:** | a point where three or more edges meet |
| **prism:** | a solid figure that has two parallel congruent bases joined by rectangular faces |
| **pyramid:** | a solid figure that has one base and triangular faces that share a vertex |

**Name each solid figure. Then write the number of faces, vertices, and edges.**

1.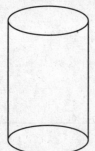

_____

_____ faces

_____ vertices

_____ edges

2.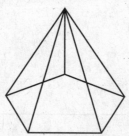

_____

_____ faces

_____ vertices

_____ edges

3.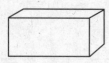

_____

_____ faces

_____ vertices

_____ edges

4.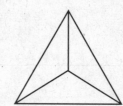

_____

_____ faces

_____ vertices

_____ edges

5.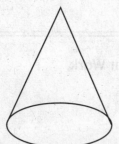

_____

_____ faces

_____ vertices

_____ edges

6.

_____

_____ faces

_____ vertices

_____ edges

## Problem Solving

**Show Your Work**

7. Alta traced the base of a solid figure. A square formed on her paper. What solid figures could she have traced?

_____

**Use with text pages 446–447.**

# Two-Dimensional Views of Solid Figures

---

### Ask Yourself

- Which view can I use to tell how the bottom layer of cubes is arranged?
- How can I use the side and top views to help me visualize the rest of the figure?

---

**Use cubes to build a three-dimensional figure with these views. Then draw the figure on triangular dot paper.**

**1.**

Top View

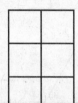
Left Side View

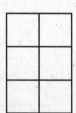
Front View

**2.**

Top View

Left Side View       Front View

**3.**

Top View

Right Side View

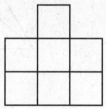
Front View

## Problem Solving

**4.** When three cubes are lined up side by side, and touching each other, how many of the faces are hidden?

**Show Your Work**

**Use with text pages 448–449.**

# Nets

**Predict what shape each net will make.**

1. 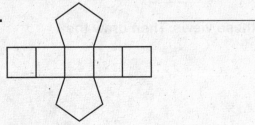 _____

2.  _____

3. 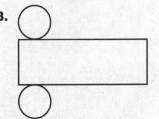 _____

4. 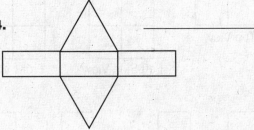 _____

**Draw a net for each solid figure.**

5.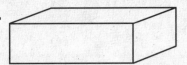

6.

7.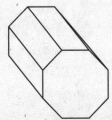

8.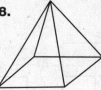

## Problem Solving

**Show Your Work**

9. Paula is making a model of a hexagonal prism. She will cut two-dimensional shapes from paper and tape them together. Identify the shapes Paula should cut to make her model.

_____

**Use with text pages 450–451.**

# Surface Area

**Determine the surface area of each solid figure.**

1. 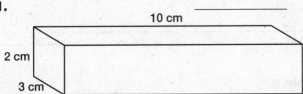 _____

2. 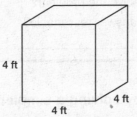 _____

3. 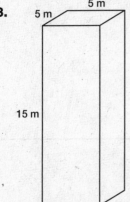 _____

4. 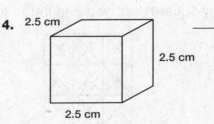 _____

**Copy and complete the table.**

| Length of One Side of Cube (s) | Area of One Face (f) | Surface Area of Cube (SA) |
|---|---|---|
| **5.** 3.5 cm | | |
| **6.** 9 cm | | |
| **7.** 15 cm | | |
| **8.** 20 cm | | |

**Problem Solving**

**Show Your Work**

9. What is the difference between a cube and a rectangular prism?

_____

**Use with text pages 452–455.**

# Problem-Solving Strategy:
# Solve a Simpler Problem

**Ask Yourself**

**Understand**  What facts do I know?

**Plan**  Did I use all the needed information?

**Solve**  Did I solve a simpler problem first?

**Look Back**  Did I solve the problem?
Is my answer reasonable?

**Solve each problem by solving a simpler problem.**

**Show Your Work**

1. How many squares can you find in the figure?

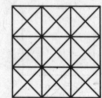

_____

_____

2. A solid figure is 6 cubes wide, 6 cubes long,
and 6 cubes high. The cube is made up of red
and green cubes. There are twice as many green
cubes as red cubes. How many red cubes does
the figure contain?

_____

_____

3. Josh built a tower with multi-colored blocks.
As he built from the ground up, he used this
pattern: red, yellow, yellow, blue. What color is
the 32nd block in Josh's tower?

_____

_____

4. Each of the 10 members of a School Board
shook hands with every other member. How
many handshakes were there?

_____

Use with text pages 456–459.

Name _____  Date _____

# Volume

| Formulas for Volume | | |
|---|---|---|
| **Volume of a Cube** | **Volume of a Rectangular Prism** | **Volume of a Triangular Prism** |
| $V = s^3$ | $V = l \times w \times h$ | $V = \frac{1}{2}(l \times w \times h)$ |

**Determine the volume of each solid figure.**

**1.** _____

5 in.
5 in.
5 in.

**2.** _____

12 m
1 m
3 m

**3.** _____

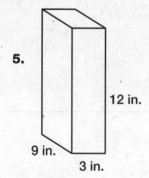

**4.** _____

8 yd
7 yd
3 yd

**5.** _____

12 in.
9 in.
3 in.

**6.** _____

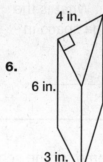

4 in.
6 in.
3 in.

## Problem Solving

**Show Your Work**

**7.** Iris' lunchbox has a volume of 300 cubic inches. If its height is 10 in. and its width is 3 in., what is its length?

_____

**117**

**Use with text pages 460–463.**

# Problem-Solving Application:
# Use Formulas

| **Ask Yourself** | |
| --- | --- |
| **Understand** | What does the question ask me to find? |
| **Plan** | Which formulas do I need to use? |
| **Solve** | Did I choose the correct formulas? |
| | Did I substitute the correct numbers for the variables? |
| **Look Back** | Did I solve the problem? |
| | Is my answer reasonable? |

**Use formulas to solve Problems 1–3.**

**Show Your Work**

1. Odessa needs to wrap a box shaped like a rectangular prism. The box is 10 in. long, 6 in. wide, and 3 in. high. How much wrapping paper does she need?

   _____

2. Akio bought a storage cube that is 4.5 ft long, 4.5 ft wide, and 4.5 ft high. What is the maximum amount of storage space in the cube?

   _____

3. A new floor has been ordered for the school's rectangular lunchroom. The length of the lunchroom is twice its width. If the lunchroom is 32 ft. wide, how many square feet of flooring were ordered?

   _____

**Use with text pages 464–467.**

# Ratios

| Ways to Write a Ratio | | |
|---|---|---|
| Word form: 1 to 3 | Ratio form: 1:3 | Fraction form: $\frac{1}{3}$ |

**Write each ratio three different ways.**

1. all shapes to triangles

   _____

| Game Pieces | Number |
|---|---|
| Rectangles | 6 |
| Triangles | 10 |
| Parallelograms | 9 |

2. parallelograms to all pieces

   _____

3. rectangles to parallelograms

   _____

4. triangles to parallelograms

   _____

5. all shapes to rectangles

   _____

6. parallelograms to triangles

   _____

7. rectangles to triangles

   _____

8. triangles to all shapes

   _____

## Problem Solving

**Show Your Work**

9. Natu has a bag of shapes. There are 5 squares, 9 triangles, and 7 circles. What is the ratio of circles to squares?

   _____

**Use with text pages 484–485.**

# Equivalent Ratios

| Different Ways to Find Equivalent Ratios | |
|---|---|
| **Way 1:** Multiply each term by the same number. $\overset{\times 5}{\frown}$ $\frac{3}{9} = \frac{6}{2} = \frac{30}{10} = \frac{6}{18}$ $\underset{\times 5}{\smile}$ | **Way 2:** Divide each term by the same number. $\frac{3}{9} = \frac{3 \div 3}{9 \div 3} = \frac{1}{3}$ |

**Write four equivalent ratios for each.**

1. $\frac{2}{5}$      2. 3:7      3. 2 to 9      4. $\frac{1}{6}$

_____ _____   _____ _____   _____ _____   _____ _____

_____ _____   _____ _____   _____ _____   _____ _____

5. 2:4      6. 4 to 7      7. $\frac{6}{5}$      8. 5 to 8

_____ _____   _____ _____   _____ _____   _____ _____

_____ _____   _____ _____   _____ _____   _____ _____

**Write each ratio in simplest form.**

9. 16:24      10. 35 to 14      11. 20:15      12. 24 to 72

_____      _____      _____      _____

13. 42:14      14. 50 to 75      15. 30:45      16. 28 to 35

_____      _____      _____      _____

**Complete each set of equivalent ratios.**

17. $\frac{8}{3} = \frac{\square}{24}$      18. $\frac{6}{21} = \frac{\square}{7}$      19. $\frac{13}{52} = \frac{1}{\square}$

_____          _____          _____

## Problem Solving

20. Three copies of a book cost $20. Write an equivalent ratio to show the cost of 9 copies.

**Show Your Work**

_____

**Use with text pages 486–487.**

# Rates

Carey can purchase 6 cans of cat food for $2. How many cans of cat food can she purchase with $10?

**Different Ways to Solve Problems Involving Rates**

**Way 1:** Use equivalent ratios.

$$\frac{6}{2} = \frac{30}{10}$$

× 5 (top), × 5 (bottom)

**Way 2:** Find the unit rate and multiply.

$$\frac{6}{2} = \frac{3}{1} \qquad \frac{3}{1} = \frac{3 \times 10}{1 \times 10} = \frac{30}{10}$$

Carey can purchase 30 cans of catfood.

## Find the unit rate.

**1.** 150 miles in 3 hours

**2.** 63 yards in 9 minutes

**3.** $2,100 in 4 weeks

_____

_____

_____

**4.** $135 in 5 hours

**5.** 21 pages in 7 hours

**6.** 642 meters in 6 minutes

_____

_____

_____

**7.** 85 drivers in 17 minutes

**8.** 120 sales in 3 hours

**9.** 98 calls in 7 minutes

_____

_____

_____

## Complete the unit rate.

**10.** 506 mi : 22 gal = _____ mi : 1 gal

**11.** $1.28 : 8 oz = _____ ¢ : 1 oz

**12.** 765 mi : 3 days = _____ mi : 1 day

**13.** $13.75 : 5 lbs = $_____ : 1 lb

**14.** $19.56 : 4 gal = $_____ : 1 gal

**15.** $31.50 : 9 tickets = $_____ : 1 ticket

## Problem Solving

**Show Your Work**

**16.** Chris can assemble a tent in 4 minutes. How many minutes will it take him to assemble 6 tents?

_____

**Use with text pages 488–491.**

Name _____   Date _____

# Proportions

┌─────────────────────────────────────────────────────┐
| **Different Ways to Solve Problems Involving Proportions** |
| **Way 1:** Use equivalent ratios. | **Way 2:** Use cross products. |
| $\frac{3}{7} = \frac{18}{\square}$ | $\frac{3}{7} \bowtie \frac{18}{n} = 3 \times n = 7 \times 18$ |
| $\frac{3}{7} = \frac{3 \times 6}{7 \times 6} = \frac{18}{42}$ | $\frac{3n}{3} = \frac{126}{3}$   $n = 42$ |
└─────────────────────────────────────────────────────┘

**Solve each proportion.**

**1.** $\frac{2}{9} = \frac{8}{p}$

**2.** $\frac{5}{7} = \frac{j}{56}$

**3.** $\frac{m}{51} = \frac{1}{3}$

**4.** $\frac{28}{r} = \frac{2}{3}$

**5.** $\frac{45}{60} = \frac{3}{n}$

**6.** $\frac{a}{12} = \frac{12}{144}$

**7.** $\frac{27}{33} = \frac{t}{11}$

**8.** $\frac{18}{b} = \frac{36}{44}$

**Write the cross products for each pair of ratios. Do the two ratios form a proportion? Write *yes* or *no*.**

**9.** $\frac{9}{11}$ $\frac{35}{44}$ _____

**10.** $\frac{5}{4}$ $\frac{60}{48}$ _____

**11.** $\frac{13}{7}$ $\frac{52}{28}$ _____

**12.** $\frac{7}{9}$ $\frac{14}{18}$ _____

**13.** $\frac{42}{88}$ $\frac{6}{11}$ _____

**14.** $\frac{9}{21}$ $\frac{30}{70}$ _____

**15.** $\frac{25}{85}$ $\frac{5}{18}$ _____

**16.** $\frac{32}{56}$ $\frac{8}{14}$ _____

## Problem Solving

**Show Your Work**

**17.** Suzu needs 24 boxes of juice for a party. A package of 3 boxes costs $0.99. Write and solve a proportion to find how much 24 boxes cost.

_____

122

**Use with text pages 492–495.**

# Similar Figures and Scale Drawings

### How to Make a Scale Drawing

**Step 1:** Write the scale as the first half of a proportion.

**Step 2:** Write and solve a proportion that shows the scale is equivalent to the length of the item in the drawing to its actual length.

$$\frac{1 \text{ cm}}{10 \text{ yd}} \longleftarrow \begin{array}{c} \text{length in drawing} \\ \text{actual length} \end{array} \longrightarrow \frac{1 \text{ cm}}{10 \text{ yd}} = \frac{12 \text{ cm}}{120 \text{ yd}}$$

**Use the scale 1 cm : 3 m to find *n* in each case.**

1. 7 cm in the drawing represents *n* m.

   _____

2. 0.25 cm in the drawing represents *n* m.

   _____

3. 0.5 cm in the drawing represents *n* m.

   _____

4. 4.5 cm in the drawing represents *n* m.

   _____

**Tell whether the rectangles in each pair are similar.**
**Explain your answers.**

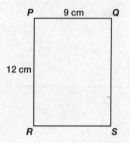

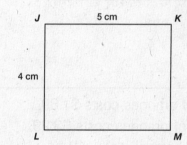

5. rectangle JKLM and rectangle PQRS  _____

6. rectangle PQRS and rectangle WXYZ  _____

7. rectangle JKLM and rectangle WXYZ  _____

## Problem Solving

8. A map scale shows 1 cm : 300 km. What is the actual distance between two towns that are 3.5 cm apart on the map?

**Show Your Work**

_____

Use with text pages 496–499.

# Problem-Solving Decisions:
# Estimates or Exact Answers

| | **Ask Yourself** |
|---|---|
| **Understand** | What question do I need to answer? |
| **Plan** | Can I use an estimate? |
| | Do I need to find an exact answer? |
| **Solve** | Which operation will I use to solve the problem? |
| **Look Back** | Did I answer the question? |

**Solve It. Tell whether you used an estimate or
an exact answer, and explain why.**

**Show Your Work**

1. A package of 15 stickers costs $2.29.
   A package of 50 stickers costs $6.59.
   Which is the better buy?

   _____

2. A 5 lb bag of oranges costs $1.89.
   An 8 lb bag of oranges costs $3.29.
   Which is the better buy?

   _____

3. Joy bought socks for $1.89 and a shirt
   for $14.98. She gave the clerk a $20 bill.
   About how much change did Joy get?

   _____

**Use with text pages 500–501.**

# Understand Percent

| Ways to Write a Percent (%) | | |
| --- | --- | --- |
| Sixty percent is written 60%. | $60\% = \frac{60}{100}$ | $\frac{60}{100} = 0.60$ or $0.6$ |

**Write each ratio as a percent.**

1. $\frac{87}{100}$

_____

2. $\frac{56}{100}$

_____

3. $\frac{29}{100}$

_____

4. $\frac{17}{100}$

_____

5. $\frac{8}{100}$

_____

6. $\frac{16}{100}$

_____

7. $\frac{38}{100}$

_____

8. $\frac{65}{100}$

_____

9. 75 parts
out of 100

_____

10. 5 parts
out of 100

_____

11. 30 parts
out of 100

_____

12. 9 parts
out of 100

_____

**Write each percent as a ratio in simplest form.**

13. 44%

_____

14. 62%

_____

15. 80%

_____

16. 77%

_____

17. 4%

_____

18. 54%

_____

19. 19%

_____

20. 1%

_____

## Problem Solving

**Show Your Work**

21. How would you show 25% on a 10 ×
10 grid?

_____

Use with text pages 506–507.

# Relate Fractions, Decimals, and Percents

**Ask Yourself**

- Did I write each percent or decimal as a ratio with a second term of 100?
- Did I write each fraction in simplest form?

**Copy and complete the table. Write each fraction in simplest form.**

| | Fraction | Decimal | Percent |
|---|---|---|---|
| 1. | | | 5% |
| 2. | | 0.55 | |
| 3. | $\frac{3}{10}$ | | |
| 4. | | 0.14 | |
| 5. | $\frac{23}{50}$ | | |
| 6. | | | 85% |
| 7. | | 0.4 | |

**Algebra** Solve each equation for *n*.

8. $\frac{21}{n} = \frac{7}{10}$

9. $\frac{n}{50} = \frac{38}{100}$

10. $n\% = \frac{19}{20}$

11. $72\% = \frac{n}{25}$

_____ _____ _____ _____

12. $n\% = \frac{1}{50}$

13. $54\% = \frac{n}{100}$

14. $92\% = \frac{n}{25}$

15. $n\% = \frac{81}{100}$

_____ _____ _____ _____

## Problem Solving

**Show Your Work**

16. There are 25 students in French class. Twelve of them are girls. What percent of the students are boys?

_____

**Use with text pages 508–509.**

# Compare Fractions, Decimals, and Percents

Compare $\frac{7}{10}$, 46%, and 0.63 to find the greatest part of a unit.

| **Way 1:** Rewrite the fraction as a decimal. | **Way 2:** Think of the percent as a number of hundredths. | **Way 3:** Compare. |
|---|---|---|
| $$\begin{array}{r} 0.7 \\ 10\overline{)7.0} \\ -7.0 \\ \hline 0 \end{array}$$ | $46\% = \frac{46}{100} = 0.46$ | $0.7 > 0.63 > 0.46$ |

**Which is the greatest?**

1. $\frac{3}{5}$  0.56  55%

_____

2. $\frac{3}{8}$  0.38  35%

_____

3. $\frac{2}{9}$  0.25  24%

_____

4. $\frac{8}{11}$  0.7  71%

_____

5. $\frac{6}{7}$  0.4  86%

_____

6. $\frac{2}{3}$  0.62  65%

_____

**Which is the least?**

7. $\frac{1}{10}$  0.11  19%

_____

8. $\frac{7}{10}$  0.63  47%

_____

9. $\frac{3}{4}$  0.71  73%

_____

10. $\frac{2}{5}$  0.42  41%

_____

11. $\frac{1}{2}$  0.52  55%

_____

12. $\frac{19}{20}$  58%  0.53

_____

**Order each set from the greatest to the least.**

13. $\frac{37}{50}$  0.8  76%

_____

14. $\frac{1}{4}$  0.31  27%

_____

15. $\frac{4}{5}$  0.65  82%

_____

## Problem Solving

**Show Your Work**

16. Forty percent of the students in an art class are 9 years old. Another 0.45 are 10 years old, and the remaining students are 11 years old. What fraction of the students are 11 years old?

_____

Use with text pages 510–513.

# Find 10% of a Number

Find 10% of 75.

| Way 1: Use a model. | Way 2: Multiply by $\frac{1}{10}$. | Way 3: Move the decimal point one place to the left to divide by 10. |
|---|---|---|
| 100% of 75 = 75 ... 10% ... $n$ | $\frac{1}{10} \times \frac{75}{1} = \frac{75}{10}$ = 7.5 | 75 ÷ 10 = 7.5 |
| To find $n$, divide 75 by 10. 75 ÷ 10 = 7.5 | | |

**Find 10% of each number.**

1. 78 _____

2. 4 _____

3. 0.27 _____

4. 315 _____

5. 19.75 _____

6. 448.9 _____

7. 641 _____

8. 200.3 _____

**Find 20% of each number.**

9. 70 _____

10. 500 _____

11. 6.28 _____

12. 18 _____

**Estimate each percent of a number.**

13. 21% of 403 _____

14. 9% of 22 _____

15. 48% of 92 _____

16. 12% of 57 _____

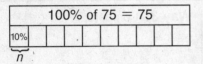 **Problem Solving**

**Show Your Work**

17. Tom went to the mall with $5.50. He spent 20% of the money on a soda. How much money is left?

_____

**Use with text pages 514–515.**

# Percent of a Number

| Different Ways to Find 55% of 60 | |
|---|---|
| **Way 1:** Write the percent as a ratio and use a proportion.<br><br>$\dfrac{55}{100} = \dfrac{n}{60}$<br><br>$55 \times 60 = 100n$<br><br>$\dfrac{55 \times 60}{100} = \dfrac{100n}{100}$<br><br>$33 = n$ | **Way 2:** Write the percent as a decimal and multiply.<br><br>$55\% = 0.55$<br><br>$0.55 \times 60 = 33$ |

**Solve by writing the percent as a ratio.**

**1.** 20% of 85     **2.** 45% of 320     **3.** 50% of 47     **4.** 30% of 200

_____     _____     _____     _____

**5.** 60% of 150     **6.** 85% of 20     **7.** 50% of 82     **8.** 24% of 40

_____     _____     _____     _____

**Solve by writing the percent as a decimal.**

**9.** 29% of 50     **10.** 18% of 300     **11.** 75% of 21     **12.** 40% of 60

_____     _____     _____     _____

**13.** 70% of 120     **14.** 55% of 70     **15.** 32% of 80     **16.** 35% of 16

_____     _____     _____     _____

**Solve. Use any method.**

**17.** 12% of 60     **18.** 15% of 30     **19.** 58% of 90     **20.** 22% of 80

_____     _____     _____     _____

## Problem Solving

**Show Your Work**

**21.** A toy car sells for $13.50. How much tax will be charged if the sales tax is 6% of the price?

_____

**Use with text pages 516–519.**

# Problem-Solving Application:
# Use Circle Graphs

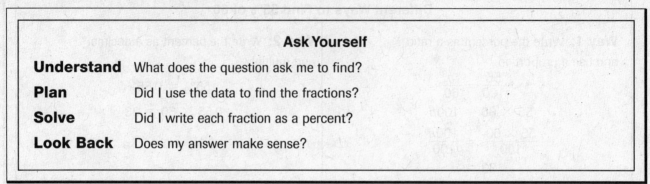

**Ask Yourself**

**Understand**  What does the question ask me to find?

**Plan**  Did I use the data to find the fractions?

**Solve**  Did I write each fraction as a percent?

**Look Back**  Does my answer make sense?

**Use the circle graph for Problems 1 and 2.**

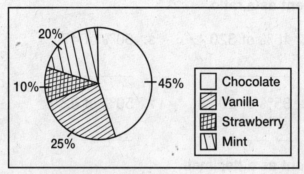

20%

10% ⊢  ⊣ 45%

25%

☐ Chocolate
▨ Vanilla
▦ Strawberry
▧ Mint

**Show Your Work**

1. Hama asked 80 people to name their favorite
   flavor of ice cream. She displayed her results in
   a circle graph. How many people chose chocolate?

   _____

2. Based on Hama's results, how many people in
   a group of 250 would likely choose strawberry?

   _____

**Use the table for Problem 3.**

| Ice Cream Shop Sales | |
| --- | --- |
| Cones | 108 |
| Sundaes | 84 |
| Milk Shakes | 48 |

3. A total of 240 customers bought items at the
   Ice Cream Shop on July 5. Make a circle graph
   to display the data as percents.

**Use with text pages 520–523.**

# Make Choices

| Different Ways to Make Choices | | |
| --- | --- | --- |
| **Make an organized list.** | **Make a tree diagram.** | **Multiply.** |
| juice, pancakes<br>juice, cereal<br>juice, eggs<br>milk, pancakes<br>milk, cereal<br>milk, eggs | juice — pancakes, cereal, eggs<br>milk — pancakes, cereal, eggs | drink choices × meal choices<br>= total<br>2 × 3 = 6 |

**You have one choice from each column. Make an organized list and a tree diagram to show all the possible choices.**

**1.**

| Outfits | | | |
| --- | --- | --- | --- |
| **Pants** | | **Tops** | |
| Tan | Black | White | Green |
| Blue | | Red | Beige |

**2.**

| Activities | |
| --- | --- |
| **Morning** | **Afternoon** |
| Swimming | Golf |
| Archery | Hiking |
| Canoeing | |

**3.**

| Frame Choices | | | |
| --- | --- | --- | --- |
| **Matte** | | **Frame** | |
| Blue | Red | Oak | Gold |
| White | Grey | Silver | Black |
| Green | | | |

**You have one choice from each category. Multiply to find the number of choices possible.**

**4.** 5 types of pie, 3 types of ice cream

**5.** 6 meats, 4 types of bread

**6.** 5 beverages, 7 desserts

_____  _____  _____

## Problem Solving

**7.** You can choose from 8 different exterior car colors and 4 different interior seat covering colors. How many possible combinations are there?

**Show Your Work**

_____

**Use with text pages 528–529.**

# Probability Concepts

The probability of an event describes the likelihood the event will occur.

Impossible         Certain

|———————————————————————————————|
0                               1
Probability                   Probability

As the probability of an event gets closer to 0, the event becomes less likely. As the probability of an event gets closer to 1, the event becomes more likely.

**You spin once on the spinner at the right. Tell which event is less likely. If necessary, describe an event as impossible or certain.**

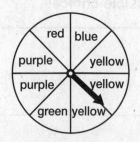

**1.** red or purple

_____

**2.** orange or brown

_____

**3.** yellow or purple

_____

**4.** green or any other color

_____

**5.** purple or blue

_____

**6.** green or orange

_____

**7.** silver or gold

_____

**8.** yellow or blue

_____

## Problem Solving

**9.** If Mack tosses a coin two times, what outcomes are possible?

_____

**Show Your Work**

**Use with text pages 530–531.**

# Theoretical Probability

> **Ask Yourself**
>
> • How many outcomes are there?
>
> • How many outcomes are favorable?
>
> • Did I express the probability as a fraction in lowest terms?

**Use the bag of shapes for Problems 1-8. If you picked one shape from the bag without looking, what would be the probability of each event? Express the probability as a fraction in simplest form.**

1.  a black triangle

    _____

2.  a square

    _____

3.  any triangle or a
    black circle

    _____

4.  a white square

    _____

5.  a dotted shape

6.  a black or white circle

    _____

7.  a white triangle

    _____

8.  not a white square

    _____

**Suppose you toss a number cube that has sides labeled 1–6.
Find the probability of each event.**

9.  a number less than 7

    _____

10. an odd number

    _____

11. a number that is greater
    than 4

    _____

## Problem Solving

12. Name an event that has a probability of $\frac{2}{7}$.

    _____

**Show Your Work**

**Use with text pages 532–535.**

# Problem-Solving Strategy:
# Make an Organized List

| | Ask Yourself | |
|---|---|---|
| **Understand** | What facts do I know? | |
| **Plan** | Did I make an organized list? | |
| **Solve** | How can I show all of the possibilities? | |
| | Do I need to cross out duplicates? | |
| **Look Back** | Did I solve the problem? | |

**Make an organized list to solve each problem.**

1. Leon, Bess, Karen, and Donna are finalists
   in a spelling bee. The top two finalists
   win trophies (without distinguishing first
   and second place). How many different
   ways can the trophies be awarded?

   _____

2. The elective classes offered at Wilson
   Middle school are cooking, wood shop,
   art, drafting, and band. Each student
   selects 3 of these classes. How many
   different groups of 3 electives are
   possible?

   _____

3. Jack, Trisha, Sam, Hoon, Chloe, and
   Sean are running for Class President and
   Vice-President. How many different pairs
   can win the election?

   _____

**Use with text pages 536–539.**

# Experimental Probability

> To find the **experimental probability** of an event, compare the number of favorable outcomes with the total number of completed trials.

**For Problems 1–2, select 4 blue cubes, 1 yellow cube, and 5 red cubes—a total of 10 cubes. Place them in a bag. Then use the recording sheet to complete each probability experiment.**

1. Find the experimental probability of selecting a blue cube. Then pick a cube, tally the result, and return the cube to the bag. Pick 20 times.

| EXPERIMENT RESULTS | | | | | |
|---|---|---|---|---|---|
| Outcome | Theoretical Probability | Prediction ? times in ? trials | Tallies | Number of Times | Experimental Probability |
| Blue | | | | | |

2. Find the experimental probability of selecting a yellow cube. Then pick a cube, tally the result, and return the cube to the bag. Pick 20 times.

| EXPERIMENT RESULTS | | | | | |
|---|---|---|---|---|---|
| Outcome | Theoretical Probability | Prediction ? times in ? trials | Tallies | Number of Times | Experimental Probability |
| Yellow | | | | | |

## Problem Solving

**Show Your Work**

3. How are theoretical probability and experimental probability alike? How do they differ?

_____

**Use with text pages 540–543.**

Name _____ Date _____

# Compound Events

---

### Ways to Find the Probability of a Compound Event

Suppose you toss a penny and roll a number cube labeled 1–6. What is the probability of the coin landing on tails, and the cube landing on an even number?

**Use a tree diagram.**

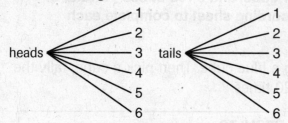

There are 12 possible outcomes and 3 favorable outcomes. $\frac{3}{12} = \frac{1}{4}$

**Use an organized list.**

| heads, 1 | tails, 1 |
|----------|----------|
| heads, 2 | tails, 2 |
| heads, 3 | tails, 3 |
| heads, 4 | tails, 4 |
| heads, 5 | tails, 5 |
| heads, 6 | tails, 6 |

There are 12 possible outcomes and 3 favorable outcomes. $\frac{3}{12} = \frac{1}{4}$

---

**Suppose you spin each spinner once. Find the probability of each compound event.**

**1.** white and 1

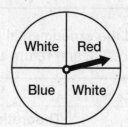

_____

**2.** red and an even number

_____

**3.** blue and a number less than 2

_____

**4.** red or white and an odd number

_____

**5.** red and a number greater than 5

_____

**6.** white and 3 or 4

_____

**7.** blue or white and a number greater than 1

_____

## Problem Solving

**8.** Use the spinners shown above to describe a compound event with a probability of 1.

_____

**Show Your Work**

**Use with text pages 544–545.**

# Problem-Solving Application: Make Predictions

**Ask Yourself**

| | |
|---|---|
| **Understand** | What does the question ask me to find? |
| **Plan** | Did I use the formula for probability? |
| **Solve** | Did I use the correct information? |
| | Did I find the probability of the event? |
| | Did I use the probability to make a prediction? |
| **Look Back** | Does my answer make sense? |

**Use the table to solve for Problems 1–2.**

**Show Your Work**

**Number of People on the Bus**

| | Bus A | Bus B |
|---|---|---|
| Girls | 22 | 8 |
| Boys | 15 | 23 |

1. What is the probability of selecting a girl at random from Bus A? Bus B?

_____

2. What is the probability of selecting a boy at random from either bus?

_____

3. Rhoda surveyed 30 classmates and found that 18 own a pet. Based on her data, how many students in a group of 500 would likely own a pet?

_____

**Use with text pages 546–549.**

# Algebra: Model Equations

> An **equation** is a mathematical sentence showing that two mathematical expressions are equal.
>
> $x + 4 = 14$ is an example of an equation.

**1.** In $x + 5 = 11$, what does $x$ represent?

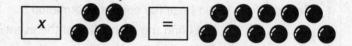

_____

**2.** Add 4 to both sides of $x + 5 = 11$. What value does $x$ represent?

_____

**3.** Subtract 2 from both sides of $x + 5 = 11$. What value does $x$ represent?

_____

**4.** In $3x = 15$, what does $x$ represent?

_____

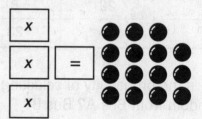

**5.** Multiply both sides of $3x = 15$ by 2. What value does $x$ represent?

_____

**6.** Divide both sides of $3x = 15$ by 3. What value does $x$ represent?

## Problem Solving

**Show Your Work**

**7.** Describe two ways of changing the equation $x + 4 = 8$ without changing the value of $x$.

_____

**Use with text pages 566–567.**

# Algebra: Write and Solve Equations

| Use Inverse Operations to Solve Equations | | | |
|---|---|---|---|
| Addition and Subtraction | | Multiplication and Division | |
| $x + 8 = 12$ | $x - 9 = 17$ | $7x = 42$ | $x \div 2 = 12$ |
| $x + 8 - 8 = 12 - 8$ | $x - 9 + 9 = 17 + 9$ | $7x \div 7 = 42 \div 7$ | $(x \div 2) \times 2 = 12 \times 2$ |
| $x + 0 = 4$ | $x - 0 = 26$ | $1 \times x = 6$ | $x \div 1 = 24$ |
| $x = 4$ | $x = 26$ | $x = 6$ | $x = 24$ |

**Solve using inverse operations.**

**1.** $t \div 7 = 10$    **2.** $52 = 4k$    **3.** $d \div 4 = 5$    **4.** $19 + b = 38$

_____    _____    _____    _____

**5.** $r - 45 = 17$    **6.** $55s = 165$    **7.** $81 \div p = 9$    **8.** $12h = 132$

_____    _____    _____    _____

**9.** $u \div 8 = 16$    **10.** $217 + c = 335$    **11.** $19q = 76$    **12.** $b - 89 = 113$

_____    _____    _____    _____

**13.** $155 + s = 249$    **14.** $r - 54 = 29$    **15.** $341 + m = 500$    **16.** $a - 99 = 176$

_____    _____    _____    _____

## Problem Solving

**Show Your Work**

**17.** What value for $a$ makes this equation
true? $5a = a$

_____

**Use with text pages 568–571.**

# Problem-Solving Strategy:
# Write an Equation

| | Ask Yourself |
|---|---|
| **Understand** | What facts do I know? |
| **Plan** | Did I write an equation? |
| **Solve** | Did I use a variable to represent what I need to know? |
| | Did I use the correct operation to solve the equation? |
| **Look Back** | Does my answer make sense? |

**Write an equation to solve each problem.**

**Show Your Work**

1. Lydia has a weekly salary of $645. This is $67 more than Dora's weekly salary. What is Dora's weekly salary?

   _____

2. Chung earned $24,720 last year. If he earned the same amount each month, what was Chung's monthly salary?

   _____

3. Leticia baby-sits for $4.50 an hour. She is saving her money for a bus ticket to a kids' Science Camp. She needs $22.50 more to pay for the ticket. How many more hours does she need to baby-sit before she has enough money?

   _____

4. Nikko is helping his dad plant a bed of tulips in front of their house. Large tulip bulbs come in bags of 6 for $7.50 a bag. They paid $150 for tulips. How many bags did they buy?

   _____

**Use with text pages 572–575.**

# Algebra: Variable and Functions

Use a function table to find values for the function, $y = 5 + x$.

- Replace $x$ in the function rule with values for $x$ from the first column of the function table. Then solve the rule for $y$.

- Remember: In a function table, there is **exactly one entry** in the second column ($y$) for every entry in the first column ($x$).

- For the function rule, $y = 5 + x$:
  If $x = 1$, then $y = 5 + 1 = 6$.
  If $x = 2$, then $y = 5 + 2 = 7$.
  If $x = 3$, then $y = 5 + 3 = 8$.
  If $x = 4$, then $y = 5 + 4 = 9$.

**Function Table**

enter
$x \rightarrow$
values

| $y = 5 + x$ | |
|---|---|
| $x$ | $y$ |
| 1 | 6 |
| 2 | 7 |
| 3 | 8 |
| 4 | 9 |

solve
for
$y$
values

**Copy and complete each function table.**

**1.** $y = 14 - x$

| $x$ | $y$ |
|---|---|
| 0 | ____ |
| 1 | ____ |
| 2 | ____ |
| 3 | ____ |

**2.** $y = 7x$

| $x$ | $y$ |
|---|---|
| 0 | ____ |
| 1 | ____ |
| 2 | ____ |
| 3 | ____ |

**3.** $y = 36 \div x$

| $x$ | $y$ |
|---|---|
| 1 | ____ |
| 2 | ____ |
| 3 | ____ |
| 4 | ____ |

## Problem Solving

**Show Your Work**

**4.** There are 8 servings in one bag of popcorn. Make a function table to show how many servings are in 2, 3, 4, and 5 bags of popcorn.

_____

Use with text pages 576–577.

# Algebra: Patterns and Functions

| Different Ways to Represent a Function | | |
|---|---|---|
| **Use a function table.** | | **Use an equation.** |

| Classes | Total Students |
|---|---|
| 1 | 24 |
| 2 | 48 |
| 3 | 72 |
| 4 | 96 |

Let $x$ = number of classes

Let $y$ = total students

$y = 24x$

**Copy and complete each function table.**

**1.** $y = 20x + 2$

| x | y |
|---|---|
| 0 | ___ |
| 1 | ___ |
| 2 | ___ |
| 3 | ___ |

**2.** $y = 35 - 2x$

| x | y |
|---|---|
| 0 | ___ |
| ___ | 29 |
| ___ | 25 |
| 7 | ___ |

**3.** $y = 6x + 13$

| x | y |
|---|---|
| 0 | ___ |
| 2 | ___ |
| ___ | 37 |
| ___ | 49 |

**Use the function table. Find the value of y for the given value of x.**

**4.** If $x = 7$, $y =$ ___

| x | y |
|---|---|
| 0 | 1 |
| 1 | 5 |
| 2 | 9 |
| 3 | 13 |

**5.** If $x = 8$, $y =$ ___

| x | y |
|---|---|
| 0 | 8 |
| 2 | 12 |
| 4 | 16 |
| 6 | 20 |

**6.** If $x = 5$, $y =$ ___

| x | y |
|---|---|
| 0 | 25 |
| 1 | 22 |
| 2 | 19 |
| 3 | 16 |

## Problem Solving

**Show Your Work**

**7.** Beth's age is 4 more than twice Jill's age. Write and solve an equation to find Jill's age if Beth is 22 years old.

_____

142

**Use with text pages 578–581.**

# Integers and Absolute Value

## Finding Absolute Value

A number's distance from zero is called its **absolute value.** What is the absolute value of ⁻6?

The absolute value of ⁻6 is 6.

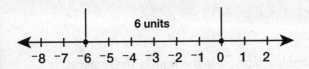 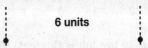

**Write the opposite of each integer.**

1. ⁻12 _____   2. ⁻5 _____   3. ⁺18 _____   4. ⁺29 _____

5. ⁺73 _____   6. ⁻92 _____   7. ⁻317 _____   8. ⁺47 _____

9. ⁻55 _____   10. ⁺118 _____   11. ⁺60 _____   12. ⁻212 _____

**Write the absolute value of each integer.**

13. 0 _____   14. ⁻16 _____   15. ⁺77 _____   16. ⁻4 _____

17. ⁺9 _____   18. ⁻15 _____   19. ⁺22 _____   20. ⁻11 _____

21. ⁺10 _____   22. ⁻24 _____   23. ⁻13 _____   24. ⁺34 _____

## Problem Solving

**Show Your Work**

25. Name a pair of integers with the same absolute value.

_____

**Use with text pages 586–587.**

Name _____  Date _____

# Compare and Order Integers

---

**Comparing Integers**

---

Order 1, ⁻2 and ⁻3 from least to greatest.

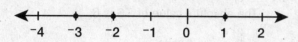

The integer farthest to the left is the least, and the integer farthest to the right is the greatest.

⁻3 < ⁻2 < ⁺1

---

**Compare. Draw a number line from ⁻8 to ⁺8 and label each integer. Write >, <, or = for each ◯.**

1. ⁺3 ◯ 0
2. ⁻1 ◯ ⁻4
3. ⁻5 ◯ ⁻1
4. ⁻2 ◯ 0

5. ⁺1 ◯ ⁺4
6. ⁻5 ◯ ⁻2
7. ⁻1 ◯ ⁻7
8. ⁺4 ◯ ⁻3

9. ⁻5 ◯ ⁻7
10. ⁻1 ◯ ⁺1
11. ⁺5 ◯ 0
12. ⁻4 ◯ ⁻6

13. 0 ◯ ⁻7
14. ⁻3 ◯ ⁺2
15. ⁺4 ◯ ⁻4
16. ⁻5 ◯ ⁻4

**Write the integers in order from least to greatest. Draw a number line if you wish.**

17. ⁻4, ⁻7, ⁻3, 0

_____

18. ⁺3, ⁻5, ⁺2, ⁻1

_____

19. ⁻12, ⁺8, ⁻9, ⁺10

_____

20. ⁺1, ⁻3, ⁻2, ⁺2

_____

---

**Problem Solving**

Show Your Work

21. At 6 A.M. the temperature in Oakville was between ⁻1°F and ⁻5°F. Name three possible temperatures in Oakville at 6 A.M.

_____

**Use with text pages 588–591.**

Name _____ Date _____

# Model Addition of Integers

Find $^-4 + {}^+5$.

**Step 1:** Use circles to show negative integers.

**Step 2:** Use squares to show positive integers.

**Step 3:** Match each circle to a square.

Since 1 square remains, the sum is positive 1.

$$^-4 + {}^+5 = {}^+1$$

**Write the addition expression shown by the circles and squares and then find the sum.**

1.

_____

2.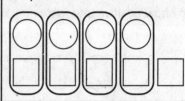

_____

**Use models to find each sum.**

3. $^+8 + {}^-6$   4. $^-7 + {}^-5$   5. $^-7 + {}^+2$   6. $^-9 + {}^+8$

_____   _____   _____   _____

7. $^+6 + {}^-10$   8. $^-11 + {}^+6$   9. $^-3 + {}^-2$   10. $^+10 + {}^-3$

_____   _____   _____   _____

**Use models to find each sum. Then compare. Write >, <, or =.**

11. $^-7 + {}^+2$ ◯ $^+1 + {}^-6$   12. $^+8 + {}^-7$ ◯ $^-10 + {}^-5$   13. $^-2 + {}^-9$ ◯ $^+15 + {}^-4$

## Problem Solving

14. At noon the temperature was 54°F. At sunset the temperature was 50°F. Write an integer to represent the change in temperature.

_____

**Show Your Work**

145

Use with text pages 592–595.

# Model Subtraction of Integers

Find $^-3 - {}^+1$.

---

**Step 1:** Use circles to show negative integers. Use squares to show positive integers.

**Step 2:** You need to subtract $^+1$ but there are no squares to take away. Add a circle and a square to show 0.

**Step 3:** Take away a square to subtract $^+1$. What is left?

Since 4 circles remain, the difference is negative 4.

$$^-3 - {}^+1 = {}^-4$$

---

**Write a subtraction expression for each. Then find the difference.**

1.

   Take away 2 squares.

   _____

2.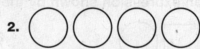

   Take away 7 circles.

   _____

**Use models to find each difference.**

3. $^+1 - {}^-5$        4. $^-2 - {}^+3$        5. $^-6 - {}^-1$        6. $^+2 - {}^-2$

_____        _____        _____        _____

7. $^+9 - {}^-11$       8. $^-7 - {}^-5$       9. $^+8 - {}^-5$       10. $^+8 - {}^-1$

_____        _____        _____        _____

11. $^+12 - {}^+9$     12. $^-11 - {}^-6$     13. $^+7 - {}^-3$     14. $^-5 - {}^+10$

_____        _____        _____        _____

## Problem Solving

15. The temperature in Amy's fish tank dropped by 2 degrees every hour. Write an integer to show how many degrees Amy's fish tank lost in 3 hours.

**Show Your Work**

_____

Use with text pages 596–597.

# Add and Subtract Integers

**Rules for Adding and Subtracting Integers**

- You can turn any subtraction expression into addition by adding the opposite
- The sum of two positive integers is positive.
- The sum of two negative integers is negative.
- The sum of a positive integer and a negative integer will have the same sign as the integer with the greater absolute value.

**Decide whether the answer will be positive or negative. Then use the number line to add or subtract.**

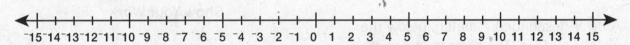

⁻15 ⁻14 ⁻13 ⁻12 ⁻11 ⁻10 ⁻9 ⁻8 ⁻7 ⁻6 ⁻5 ⁻4 ⁻3 ⁻2 ⁻1 0 1 2 3 4 5 6 7 8 9 10 11 12 13 14 15

**1.** $0 + {}^+6$     **2.** ${}^-3 - {}^-11$     **3.** ${}^-9 + {}^+1$     **4.** ${}^+6 - {}^-4$

_____    _____    _____    _____

**5.** ${}^-11 - {}^+4$     **6.** ${}^-12 + {}^+8$     **7.** ${}^+3 - {}^-6$     **8.** ${}^+4 + {}^-7$

_____    _____    _____    _____

**9.** ${}^+6 + {}^-9$     **10.** ${}^-12 - {}^-5$     **11.** ${}^-5 + 0$     **12.** ${}^+8 - {}^-2$

_____    _____    _____    _____

## Problem Solving

**Show Your Work**

**13.** Stacey got on an elevator and rode up 3 floors, then down 5 floors and got off. If she got off on the sixth floor, where did she enter the elevator?

_____

**Use with text pages 598–601.**

# Problem-Solving Application:
# Use Integers

| | Ask Yourself |
|---|---|
| **Understand** | What does the question ask me to find? |
| **Plan** | Did I record the correct information? |
| **Solve** | Did I use positive and negative integers? |
| | Did I use a number line or counters to solve the problem? |
| **Look Back** | Did I check my answer by working through the problem? |

**Solve.**

**Show Your Work**

1. A diver descended 7 meters below the water's surface. The diver then swam down another 4 meters. What integer shows the diver's position in relation to the water's surface?

   _____

2. A bus left the station with 30 riders. At the first stop, 7 riders left the bus and 3 got on. At the second stop, 8 riders left the bus and 2 got on. What integer shows the number of riders after the second stop in relation to the original number of riders?

   _____

3. Peg stood at a starting line. She then moved 5 steps backward, 2 steps forward, and 3 steps backward. What integer shows her position in relation to the starting line?

   _____

**Use with text pages 602–605.**

# Integers and the Coordinate Plane

- In a coordinate plane, the horizontal axis is called the *x*-axis and the vertical axis is called the *y*-axis.
- The axes divide the grid into 4 quadrants, numbered I, II, III, and IV.
- Every point on a coordinate plane is named by an ordered pair, (*x*, *y*).
- The point named by the ordered pair (0, 0) is the origin.

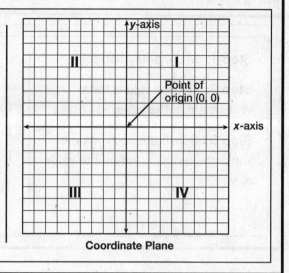

Coordinate Plane

**Use the graph for Problems 1–12. Write the ordered pair for each point.**

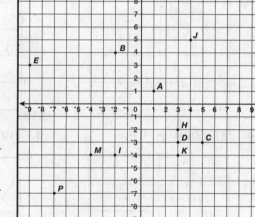

**1.** I _____

**2.** A _____

**3.** C _____

**4.** B _____

**5.** P _____

**6.** H _____

**Write the letter name for each point.**

**7.** (⁻9, ⁺3) _____

**8.** (⁺4, ⁺5) _____

**9.** (⁺3, ⁻4) _____

**10.** (⁻4, ⁻4) _____

**11.** (⁻3, ⁺9) _____

**12.** (3, ⁻3) _____

## Problem Solving

**Show Your Work**

**13.** If you plotted the points (⁻3, ⁻3), (⁻3, ⁺3), (⁺3, ⁺3), and (⁺3, ⁻3) and connected the points in that order, what shape would form?

_____

**Use with text pages 610–613.**

# Integers and Functions

$y = 3x - 4$

**Step 1:** Make a function table.

**Step 2:** Choose values for $x$.
Write them in the table.

**Step 3:** Substitute each value of
$x$ into the function to find the value
of $y$.

If $x = 1$, then $y = 3(1) - 4 = {}^-1$
If $x = 2$, then $y = 3(2) - 4 = 2$
If $x = 3$, then $y = 3(3) - 4 = 5$
If $x = 4$, then $y = 3(4) - 4 = 8$

**Function Table**

| x | y |
|---|---|
| 1 | ⁻1 |
| 2 | 2 |
| 3 | 5 |
| 4 | 8 |

**Complete the function table.**

**1.** Function: $y = x + 4$

| x | y |
|---|---|
| ⁻3 | |
| ⁻2 | |
| ⁻1 | |
| 0 | |

**2.** Function: $y = x - 3$

| x | y |
|---|---|
| ⁻2 | |
| 0 | |
| 2 | |
| 5 | |

**3.** Function: $y = 6 - x$

| x | y |
|---|---|
| ⁻2 | |
| ⁻1 | |
| 0 | |
| 3 | |

**4.** Function: $y = 4x$

| x | y |
|---|---|
| 0 | |
| 1 | |
| 2 | |
| 3 | |

**5.** Function: $y = x - 6$

| x | y |
|---|---|
| ⁻3 | |
| 0 | |
| 3 | |
| 6 | |

**6.** Function: $y = 7x$

| x | y |
|---|---|
| 0 | |
| 1 | |
| 2 | |
| 3 | |

## Problem Solving

**Show Your Work**

**7.** The first two set of ordered pairs in
a function table are $({}^-3, {}^-2)$ and
$({}^-2, {}^-1)$. What is the function?

_____

**Use with text pages 614–615.**

# Algebra: Use Functions and Graphs

| How to Graph an Equation | |
| --- | --- |
| **Step 1:** Make a function table to find the ordered pairs. | **Step 2:** Graph each ordered pair. |

**Find the values of _y_ to complete each function table. Then graph each equation on grid paper.**

**1.** Function: $y = 4x - 2$

| x | y |
| --- | --- |
| 0 | |
| 1 | |
| 2 | |
| 3 | |

**2.** Function: $y = 3x + 2$

| x | y |
| --- | --- |
| 0 | |
| 1 | |
| 2 | |
| 3 | |

**Find three ordered pairs in the first quadrant for each function. Then use them to graph the function.**

**3.** $y = 8x$

**4.** $y = 2x + 5$

**5.** $y = 3x - 4$

**6.** $y = x + 3$

_____  _____  _____  _____

## Problem Solving

**Show Your Work**

**7.** Ian said it is possible to determine if two points lie along the same vertical line by simply looking at their ordered pairs. Do you agree with Ian? Tell why or why not.

_____

**Use with text pages 616–619.**

# Problem-Solving Application:
# Use a Graph

**Ask Yourself**

**Understand** What do I need to find?

**Plan** Did I record the correct information?

**Solve** What patterns do I see?

**Look Back** Is my answer reasonable?

---

**Solve. Use the table for Problems 1–2.**

**Show Your Work**

| Students | 100 | 200 | 300 | 400 |
|----------|-----|-----|-----|-----|
| Teachers | 7 | 12 | 17 | 22 |

1. As the number of students at Middlecreek Elementary grew, the school hired more teachers. Write an equation to show the relationship between teachers (*t*) and students (*s*) at the school.

   _____

   _____

2. Solve the equation to find the number of teachers when 600 students attend the school.

   _____

   _____

**Solve. Use the graph for Problems 3–4.**

3. Write an equation for the data shown in the graph using *s* for students and *c* for candy sold.

   _____

   _____

4. Solve the equation to find how much candy 100 students would sell.

   _____

   _____

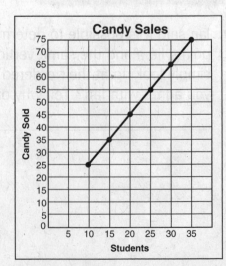

**Use with text pages 620–621.**

Name _____  Date _____

# Transformations in the Coordinate Plane

- A **transformation** is a change in the position of a figure on a graph.
- A **reflection** is a flip of a figure that results in a mirror image.
- A **rotation** is a turn around a given point. One complete turn is 360°.
- A figure has **rotational symmetry** if it looks exactly the same after being rotated less than 360° around a center point.

**Use the diagram. Name the coordinates of triangle ABC after the transformations.**

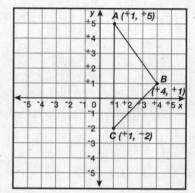

1. Reflect over the *y*-axis.

_____

2. Translate right 1, then down 2

_____

3. Rotate $\frac{1}{4}$ a turn around (0, 0)

_____

4. Translate left 3, then up 1

_____

**Write *line*, *rotational*, or *both* to describe the symmetry of the figure.**

5.

_____

6.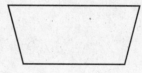

_____

## Problem Solving

**Show Your Work**

7. If a point is located at (−1, −1) and it shifts up 1 and to the right 1, where it is now located?

_____

Use with text pages 622–625.